REBECCA GABRIEL

Appearances

Experimental Portraiture

Rebecca Gabriel

For Jonah

without you, none of this would have been possible

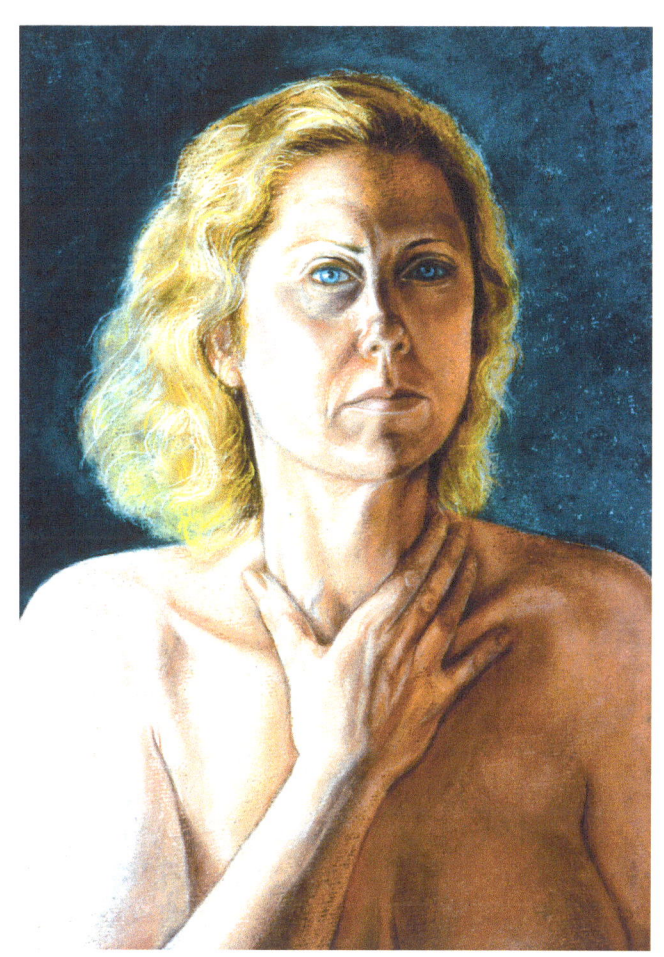

ISBN: 978-1-930835-28-3

Introductory page: *Self Portrait with Hand*. Pastel on paper, 29" x 24"
Title page: *Elegy for Sharon*, detail. Oil on canvas, 30" x 17"

Photo credits: Rob Jaffe, Painted Pixel

www.wellstonepress.com

Appearances

Experimental Portraiture

Rebecca Gabriel

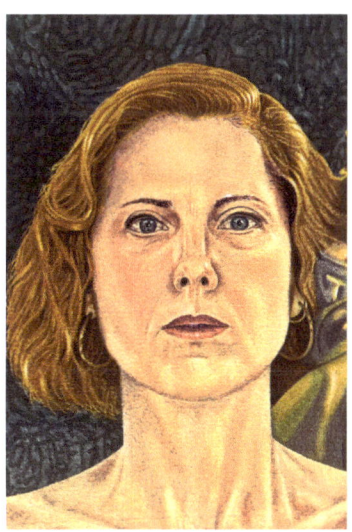

Introduction by John Seed

Wellstone Press

Denver, Colorado

Contents

Preface

ALL OF THE ARTWORKS in this book begin with a traditional portrait drawing or painting. Often, years pass before the initial piece is altered. At times, I irrevocably erase or paint out areas. In other instances, I resort to cutting up paintings or drawings in order to collage or create a new stand-alone piece. All this risk-taking is done in the hopes of creating something stronger and more authentic.

This type of destruction of my original work feels not only perilous, but also limiting. Thus, I gratefully welcome using New Media prints, as proxies. At times, I feel it necessary to permanently alter the original piece, but for the most part I use New Media prints on paper or canvas. This allows me the freedom to experiment, fail, and push the boundaries of traditional portraiture.

One approach is to utilize these printed portraits in conjunction with maps, diagrams, collage, and even dirt... This experimental modality might also transition into using high flow paint in partnership with the portrait. The high flow surfaces serve as a background or a direct pour across the portrait itself. I also employ ready-made papers, which bring a new aesthetic to my work. I use these extraordinary papers as dynamic portrait backgrounds.

Overall, in creating these new works, I fortunately am able to incorporate the best of both worlds. I combine my "Old Master" egg tempera and oil painting technique with digital printing, collage, and high flow paint. I also merge my proclivity for realism and control with my pension for multiple interpretations and chance. My intention is for a synergy to occur between tradition and experimentation, perhaps resulting in a fresh and unique perspective.

In creating portraits, I am acutely aware of the many aspects of individuals—both overt and mysterious. Moods are in constant flux, and each of us is challenged by circumstance. My hope is that these portraits honor these many complexities, as they honor those I have been able to portray.

My creative exploration and sensibility is the binding that holds these pages together—a story that has no plot, no conclusion, and is not linear.

– Rebecca Gabriel

Introduction

Rebecca Gabriel: None of This is Conscious

John Seed

ARTIST REBECCA GABRIEL, grew up in what she calls a "psychoanalytical family," in Los Angeles, California. As a result, she was encouraged to develop and understand her own inner consciousness, so much so, that as a child, Gabriel started analyzing her own dreams while sleeping. Given this background, it is not surprising that her artwork—even her "conventional" portraits—has always emanated distinct psychological undercurrents. In Gabriel's sensibility, there is always more going on than the eyes can see.

Interested in drawing from a young age, Gabriel attended UCLA at a time when representational art had been eclipsed by abstraction. While studying there—and taking classes from Jan Stussy and Tony Berlant—she remembers being shocked one day when an instructor told her that her work was "heavy-handed." Thinking about it later, Gabriel realized that she was trying to fit into the current artistic *zeitgeist*, by making gestural "art marks." It wasn't until after graduation, when she spent time in a village in Denmark, with her first husband and mentor, the artist and art critic, Robert C. Morgan, that Gabriel found her "true north." She emerged a realist, with a contemporary eye. Diligent, highly skilled, and especially interested in depicting women, Gabriel has built an oeuvre that leans towards inner exploration and resists flattering her subjects.

Gabriel's recent series, "Extractions," uses a remarkably straightforward approach—extracting key elements from previous works—to refocus and emphasize a central emanation. For example, *Heart*, which was extracted from a half-length female figure titled *The Hybrid*, moves in for an unflinching view of an anatomically correct heart on view outside a woman's chest. It is an uncomfortable image that generates many questions for viewers. For example, does the heart symbolize mortality, feeling, or both? In some respects, *Heart* is a Surrealist painting that stands for a kind of dreaming, that painting makes visible. It also serves as a metaphor for interiority, one of Gabriel's lifelong concerns.

The Soldier is an example from Gabriel's series "X-Rays" in which the bodies of her subjects reveal hidden symbols displayed with a kind of clinical clarity. The soldier has death literally on his mind in the form of a small curving skeleton. In this piece, the muscular young man closes his eyes, and it seems, he carries his consciousness of mortality with a certain acceptance. The grave simplicity of this painting, set in an indeterminate grey space, balances the subject's dignity and vulnerability. The effect of this solemnity is that the painting transmits a certain air of sainthood that can also be found in the works of Ribera or Zurbarán.

Gabriel's "Mutations" series uses Xerox and collage elements overlaid with sketches to generate authentic responses to internal mysteries. They represent a moving forward in her work—and in her personal process— towards a more ambiguous model of expression. In *Passage*, a drawing of the artist's mother appears in a grove of peacock feathers. Her closed eyes and aged features work both with and against the flowing lines and bold "blue eye" that make the crowd of feathers feel almost alive. Other works in the series feature Gabriel's husband, the poet Jonah Bornstein, juxtaposed with maps and diagrams that introduce unconscious maps redolent of time and experience.

The considerable body of work that Gabriel calls "High Flow" represents an artistic breakthrough. The plumed and flowing settings of these portraits provides a generative and flexible set of unconscious suggestions. Double images (as in *Twins*) and wavelike rhythms (as in *Ghost*) create both a sense of drama and change. In these works, and the Suminagashi and decorative paper collages that have accompanied them, Gabriel has entered a new phase of perceptual painting that draws from a wide range of sources gleaned from both art and nature. They offer a mature artist's reflections on a Faustian revelation: the more we know the more we are aware of what we don't know. That paradox has been at the heart of Gabriel's work all along, but in her recent work it is more active and expansive than ever.

Finding ways to try and express the mysteries of others through portraiture has taken Rebecca Gabriel towards her own imaginative core. Her journey has been very rich indeed as she has inched closer and closer to things that will never be understood.

Foreword

Rebecca Gabriel

DURING MY FORMATIVE YEARS as an art student, I discovered that my penchant to explore seemingly endless options, was (at the time) a liability, not an asset. In working, I often fell down a rabbit hole of embellishment and reconfiguration. Recognizing the danger of "limitless" possibilities, shaped my artistic decisions for many decades.

At that early juncture, I set aside my confusing and failed explorations for a more specific, singularly focused technique. The creative doors that opened were direct and in harmony with my chosen representational subject. I had faith in the psychological and creative possibilities that would emerge by using this restrained and intentional focus.

Through the Naropa Institute, I also studied Old Master painting techniques in Austria, using egg tempera and oil. Thus, my technical knowledge grew. I became more adept and committed to this traditional methodology in painting the figure and other subjects. Much of this work is represented in my earlier book, *Woman's Journey—A Life in Painting*, also published by Wellstone Press in 2008.

However, as I worked on these carefully executed pieces, which often took many months, other trajectories and possibilities kept murmuring seductively in my ear. Were these whisperings legitimate or something wanton, trying to distract me from my singular purpose? I ignored these tugs of possibility because I had a lingering fear that I might lose my way and/or ruin my work.

It wasn't until I received the Haines Foundation Grant in 2014, awarded specifically to support these renegade musings, that I finally decided to fully surrender to these persistent and alternative enticements.

Thus, I began the "Mutations" series, exploring the multi-faceted and protean "truths" of my subjects. Because I was using New Media prints on both paper and canvas, I felt emboldened about the outcome, as I wasn't going to ruin any one-of-a-kind original.

At last, I was able to return to my early inclination to explore and plumb my subjects from many angles. I began employing collage, super-impositions, high flow paint, Suminagashi and decorative papers, intense cropping, juxtapositions, and overlays, as well as secondary imagery. All this was in partnership with my original drawings, pastels, and paintings. This freedom unleashed a new body of artwork, *Appearances*, which I have brought together in this book. This work includes the following series: "Extractions," "X-Rays," "Mutations," "High Flow Portraits," and "Suminagashi & Decorative Paper Collage."

Like nesting Russian dolls, I often realized that when I released an image, another image rested within, waiting to be born.

With this book, I hope to reveal a new perspective, in not only the process, but also its manifestation.

I think of this body of work as a dance, with a variety of steps and rhythms, responding to a refrain that moves through my being.

Song of Myself, 51

Walt Whitman

The past and present wilt—I have fill'd them, emptied them.
And proceed to fill my next fold of the future.
Listener up there! what have you to confide to me?
Look in my face while I snuff the sidle of evening,
(Talk honestly, no one else hears you, and I stay only a minute longer.)
Do I contradict myself?
Very well then I contradict myself,
(I am large, I contain multitudes.)
I concentrate toward them that are nigh, I wait on the door-slab.
Who has done his day's work? who will soonest be through with his supper?
Who wishes to walk with me?
Will you speak before I am gone? will you prove already too late?

Chapter 1

Extractions

ALL OF THE PIECES in this series sprung from details extricated from larger works. Various approaches include: New Media prints, newly created oil paintings, and collages, using both prints and/or original components. Let me explore some of these processes.

One approach is to extract a key element from a previous work. Simply, these extracted pieces become separate and complete entities—with their own focus and power.

For example, in the work *Heart*, I extracted a detail from the original piece, *The Hybrid* (p. 32), creating a separate and simpler piece using New Media printing. This work reveals its own poetic urgency, using the dynamic relationship among the hand, breast, and heart.

Another approach is to create a separate and new painting also based on a previous composition. For instance, the piece *Piper* is an original painting, but the composition and idea for the piece emerged from an earlier work called *Alex*. This earlier piece is a basic portrait. I determined that by severe cropping of the face, I might realize a fresh and perhaps more expressive composition. Thus, I painted *Piper* in egg tempera and oil paint on panel. Due to the extreme cropping, this piece verges on abstraction, while synthesizing a strong level of realism and emotional impact.

In *Sisters*, I cut out a large area of a previous oil painting, *The Message*. I collaged this remnant together with a New Media print on canvas. This New Media print was also extracted, but from a different larger oil painting, *The Visitation*. This process uses components from two separate original oil paintings to create the piece *Sisters*. In this work, portions of both an original oil painting and a New Media canvas print are brought together and reworked accordingly.

In conclusion, the "Extractions" series, in certain cases, involves creating an entirely new painting, as in *Piper*. In other instances, I might cut up an original painting, using it as a component in a new collage composition, such as *Sisters*. In other cases, however, I have kept the original piece intact, extracting New Media prints on canvas and/or paper, in works like *Heart* and *Hand On Throat*. In other works, for example *Refugee*, I have combined several of these processes using traditional media, collage, and New Media.

In life, as in art, much ado may surround a poignant kernel of meaning, like the opening of a single flower. When all else falls away, there may exist a new clarity, and a fresh singular image. However, sometimes, like metal filings to a magnet, other components attach, to bring forth new constellations and works of art.

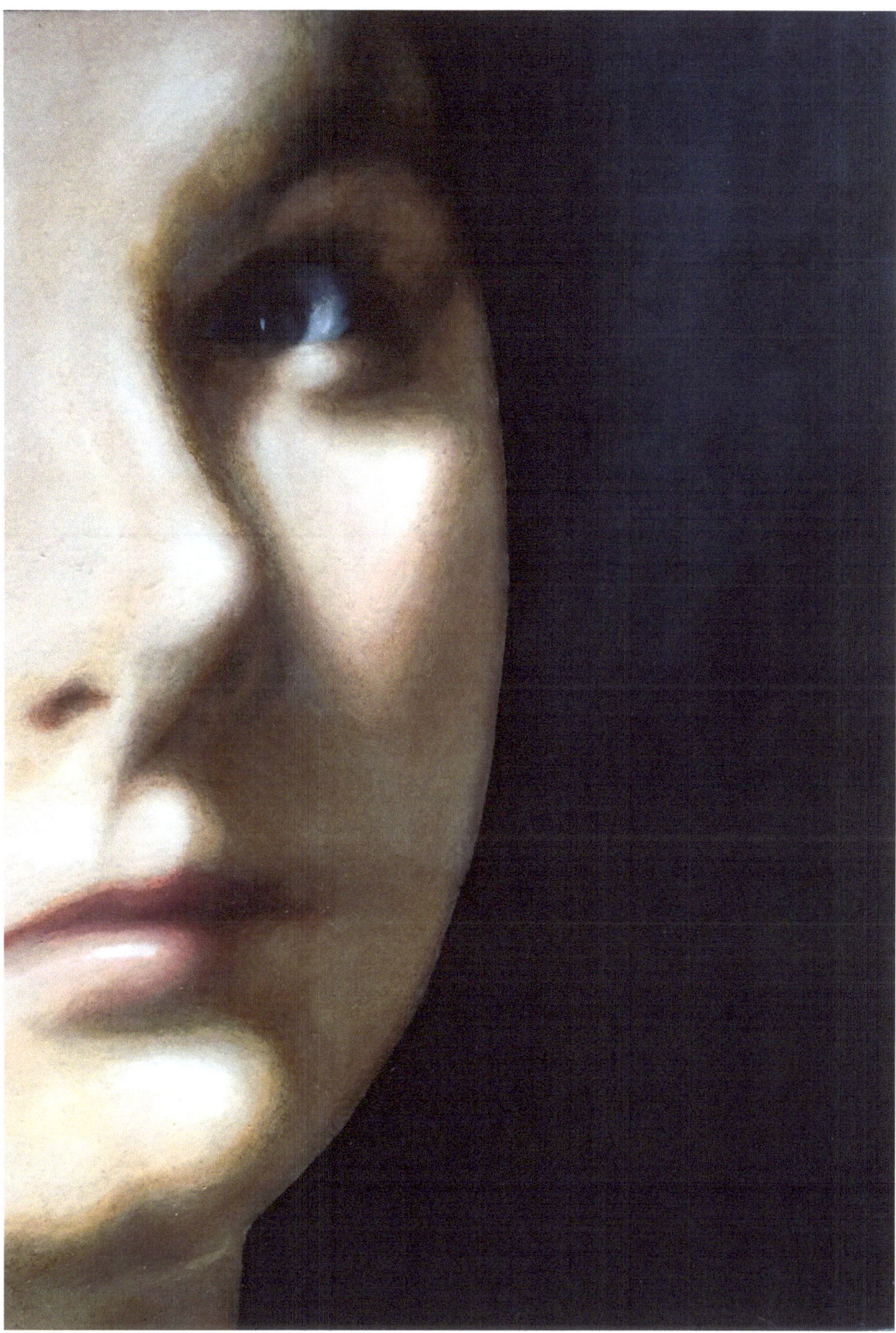

Piper
oil and egg tempera on panel
12" x 9"

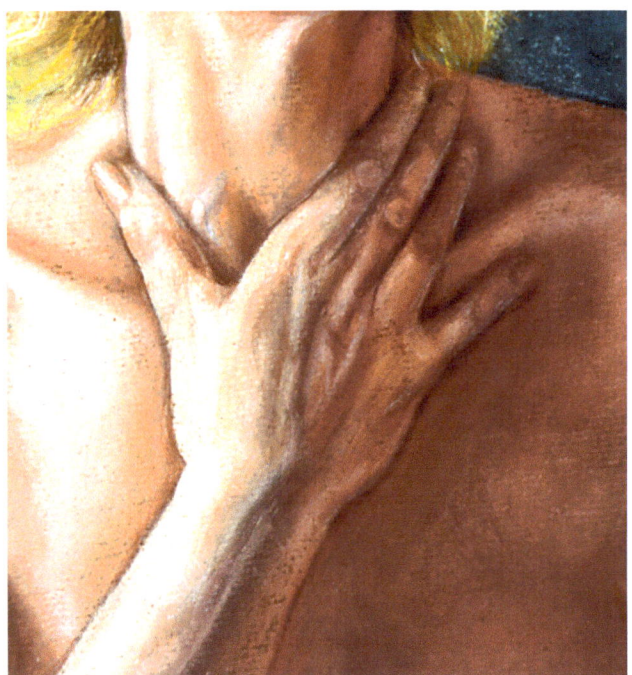

Hand On Throat
pastel, New Media
20" x 16"

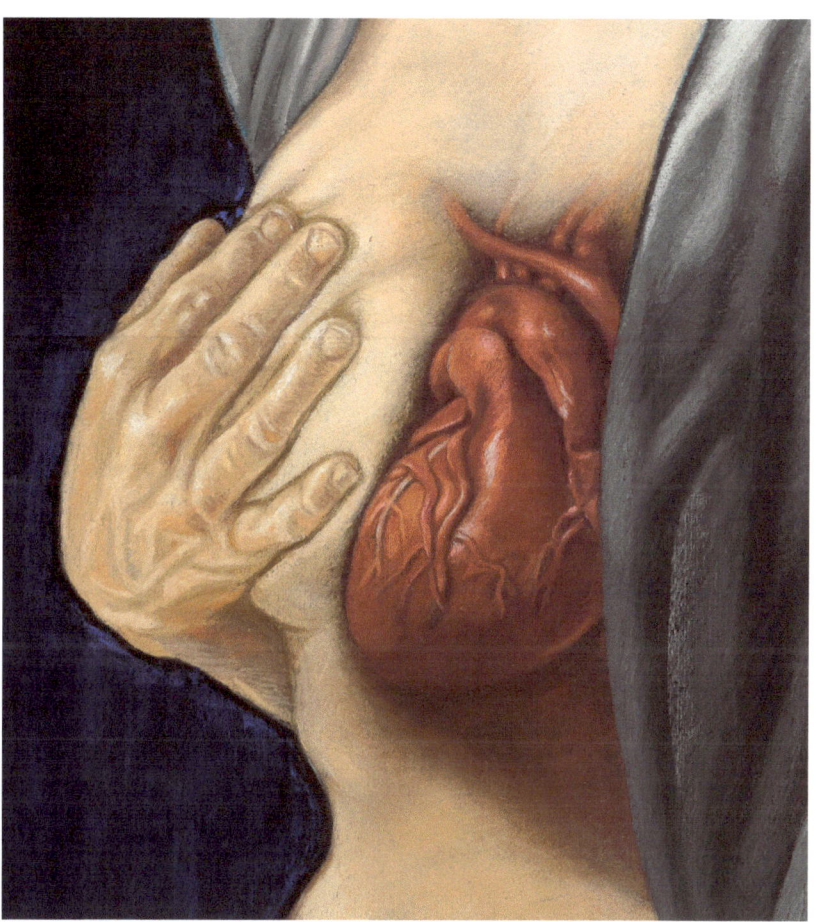

Heart
pastel, New Media
18" x 16"

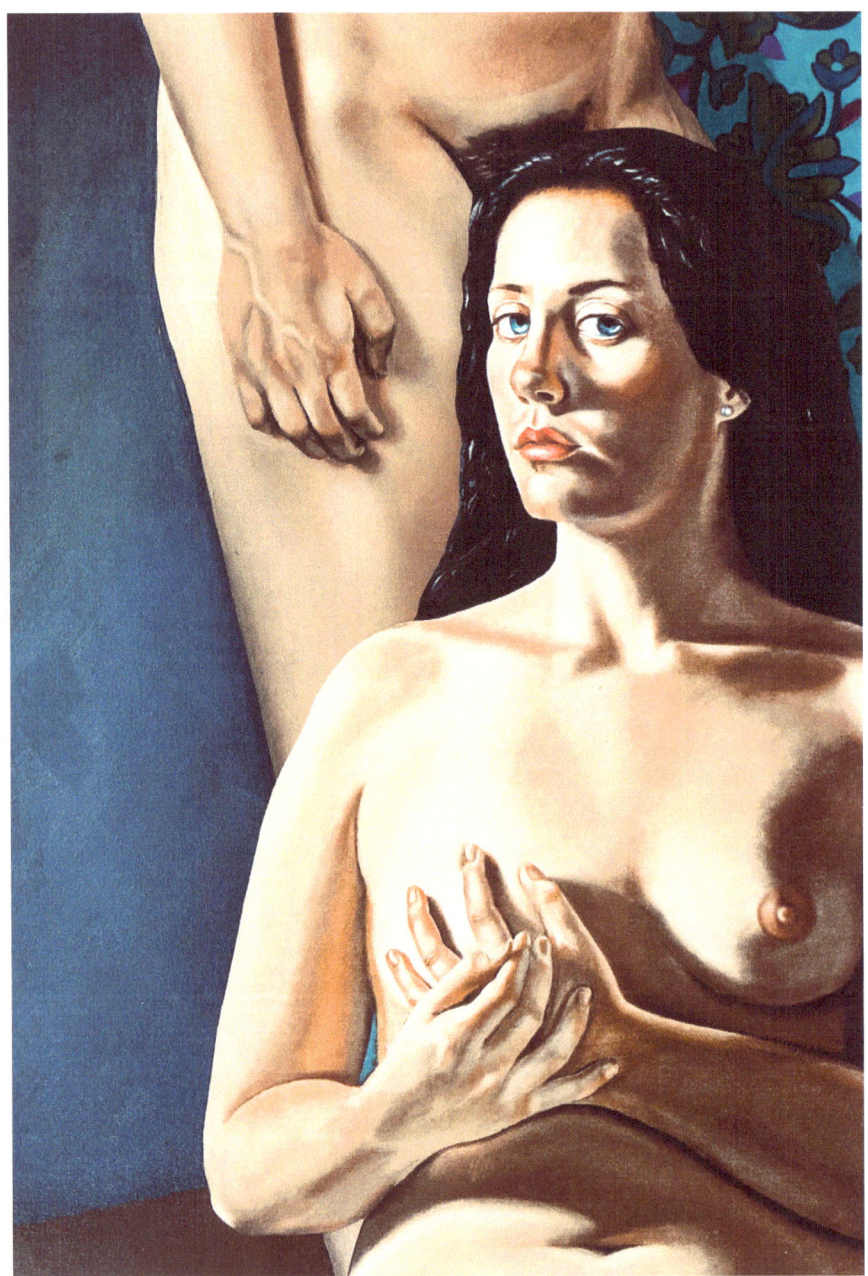

Sisters
oil, New Media, collage, acrylic on canvas
33" x 20"

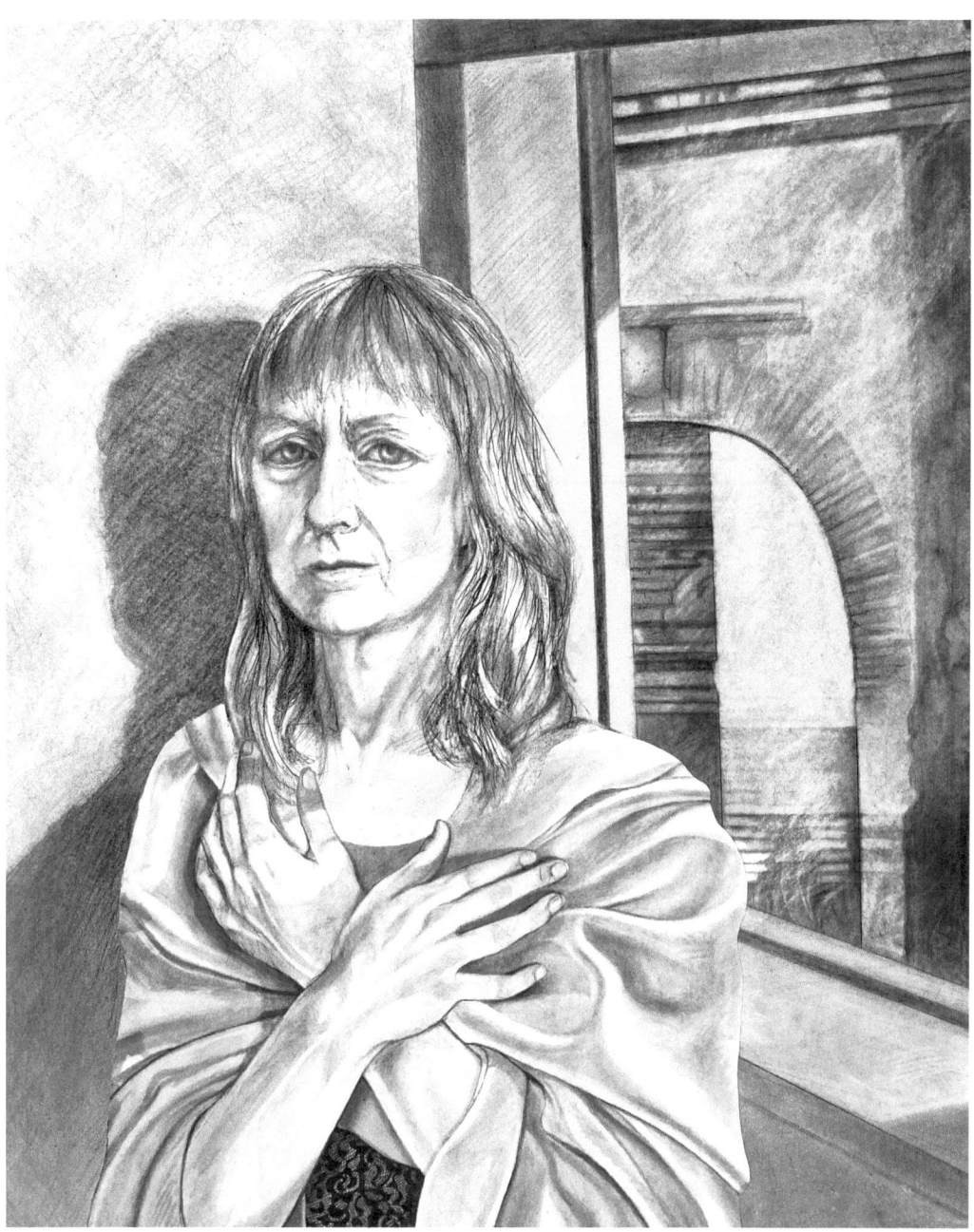

Refugee
pencil, New Media, collage
15" x 14"

Chapter 2

X-Rays

THESE WORKS FUSE or amalgamate a representational image with something unexpected. I begin with the figure and then expose an element beneath the surface of flesh and bone, a kind of window into the subject, both literally and psychologically.

For example, in *The Soldier*, a portion of the skull is removed, creating an aperture into the brain cavity. Within this recess, a skeleton rests in a fetal position, curled as if in a womb. The man's eyes are shut, as he manifests thoughts of mortality.

Mindset resembles *The Soldier*, as the interior of the brain cavity is also exposed. However, what is revealed is a fetus, also curled and resting within the young woman's mind. Like *The Soldier*, her eyes are shut. She is concentrating on this unborn baby. The young woman is perched on the edge of something. Her expression is one of emotional resolve. The shapes within her ear echo the form of the fetus, and a viewer might sense she is also "listening" to the baby's presence. Her body is thin and nubile, with no visible hint of pregnancy. The image lends itself to interpretation.

In *The Hybrid*, the subject's chest cavity is open, exposing the organ of her heart. It is as if the heart itself is her other breast. The subject's hand simultaneously cradles and also pulls at her own breast to frame and reveal her beating heart. Emotionally the portrait combines the elements of wariness and vulnerability, while an orb of both protection, power, and receptivity surround the subject's head.

All of these pieces are executed in pastel—for me the most flexible and forgiving medium. Using pastel, ideas can be shaped, erased, and reshaped, which leads the way to these explorations.

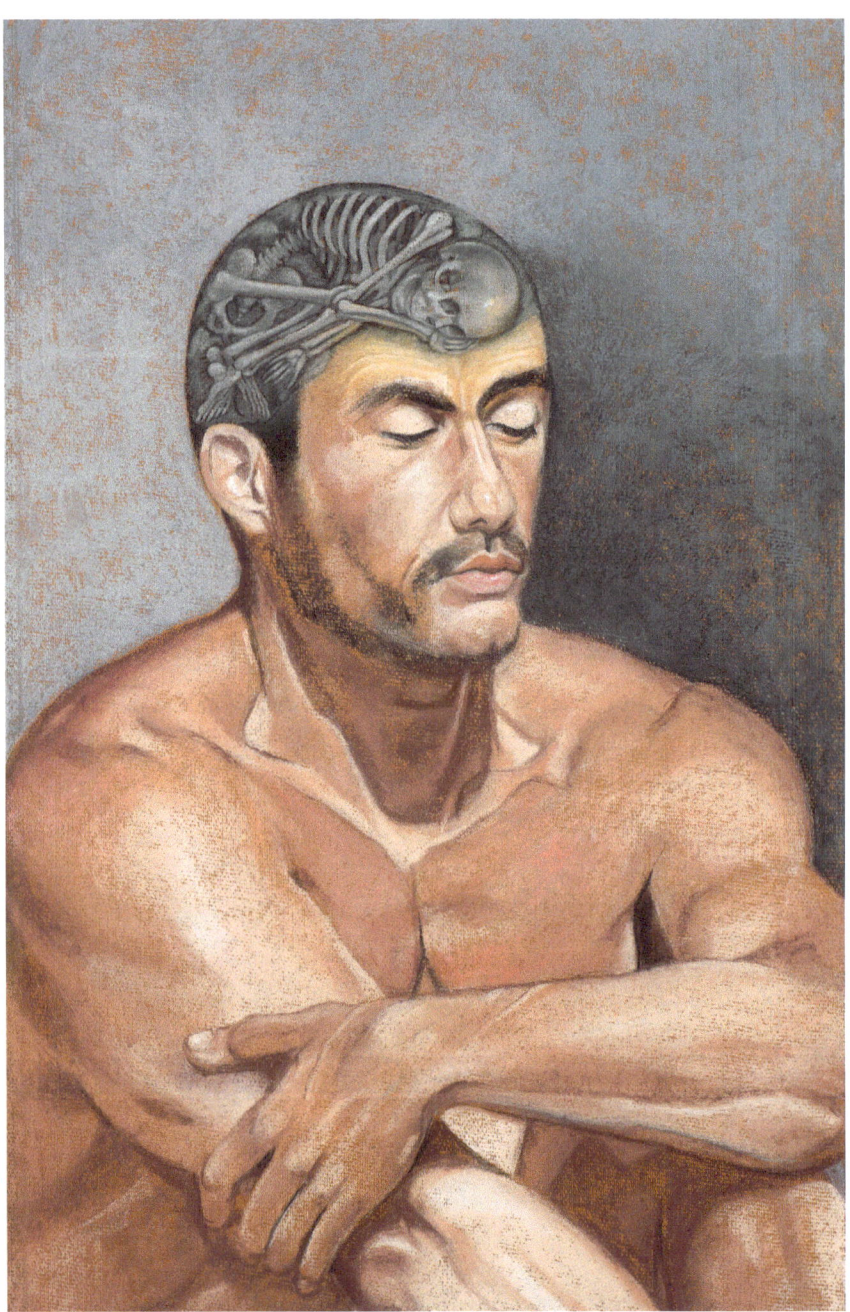

The Soldier
pastel on paper
31" x 19"

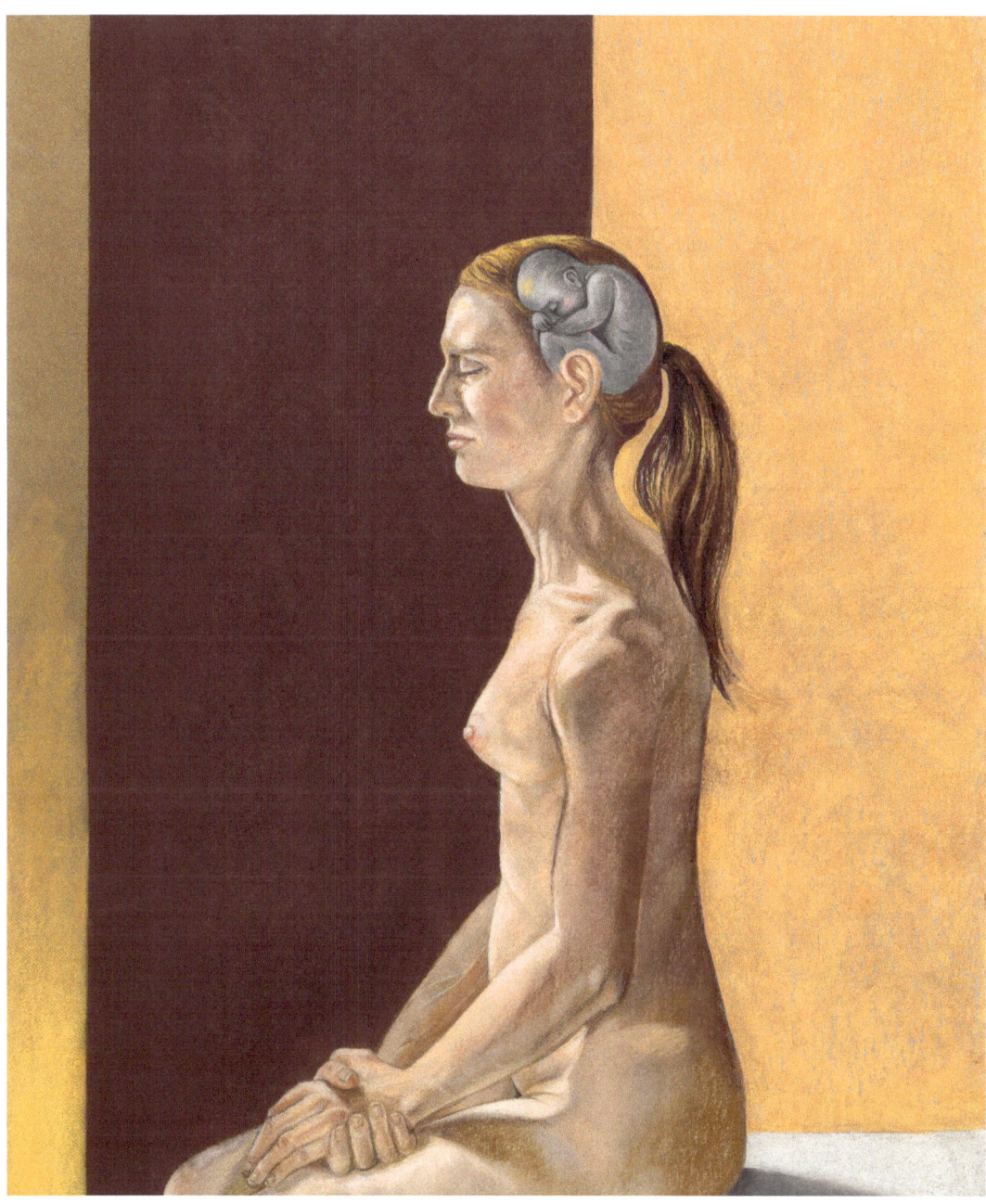

Mindset
pastel on paper
41" x 32"

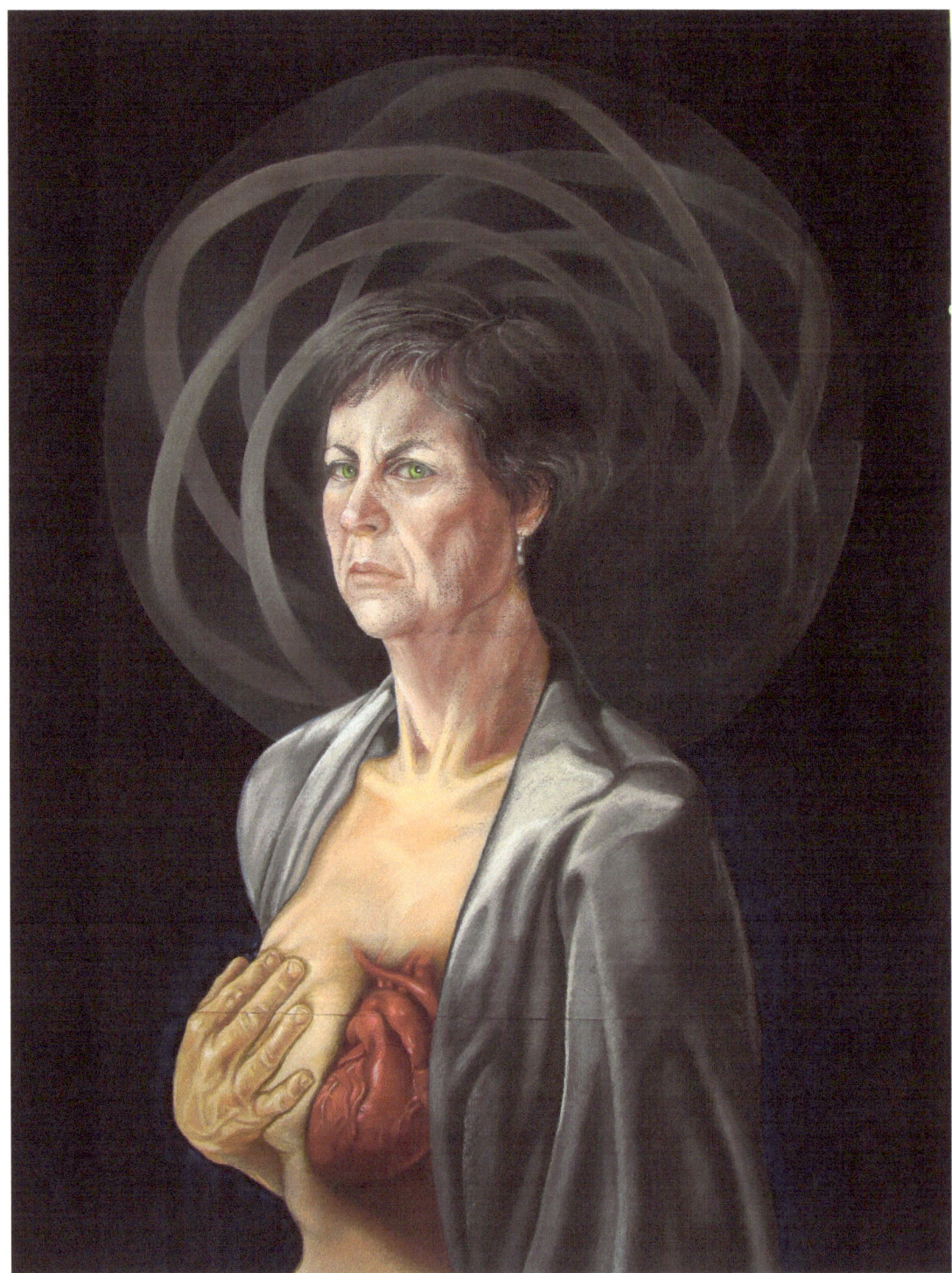

The Hybrid
pastel on paper
30" x 22"

Chapter 3

Mutations

THIS SERIES IS THE BRIDGE, in my portraiture, to greater experimentation. In these pieces, I am able to remove the preciousness of my original work, and begin to investigate more freely using reproduced images of my sketches. This approach flung the proverbial window open, and out I flew, alighting on concept after concept.

I use a variety of printing techniques, collage, resource materials, layered Xeroxes, and more. As I explore the honeycomb of new resources and creativity, I have, uncharacteristically, come to relish the failures, alongside the successes.

In this process, I am in partnership with accident and juxtaposition. For example, the sketch of my mother used in *Passage*, was inadvertently run through a defective copy machine. The machine pulled and distorted the image, echoing her otherworldly quality and evoking the inevitable pull of her final passing.

Thus, "Mutations" has let a creative genie out of the bottle, allowing me to follow new directions without hesitation.

I will share the evolution of *Disinterred* as an example of my experimental process. After my mother passed, I crumpled a copy of a drawing of her, unfolded it carefully, streaked it with conte crayon, then buried it for several days, which happened to include rainfall. I carefully unearthed and opened the crumpled drawing, now imprinted with particles of dirt and watermarks across her face. In this portrait, I perhaps discovered the pathos and truth of my grief.

With a sketch of my husband, I used a variety of maps and schematic drawing resources. I then superimposed the sketch of his face over these elaborate constellations of place and geometry. Why did I join my husband's face to these maps and complex structures? I don't fully understand, except I felt it was an authentic coupling with his mystery.

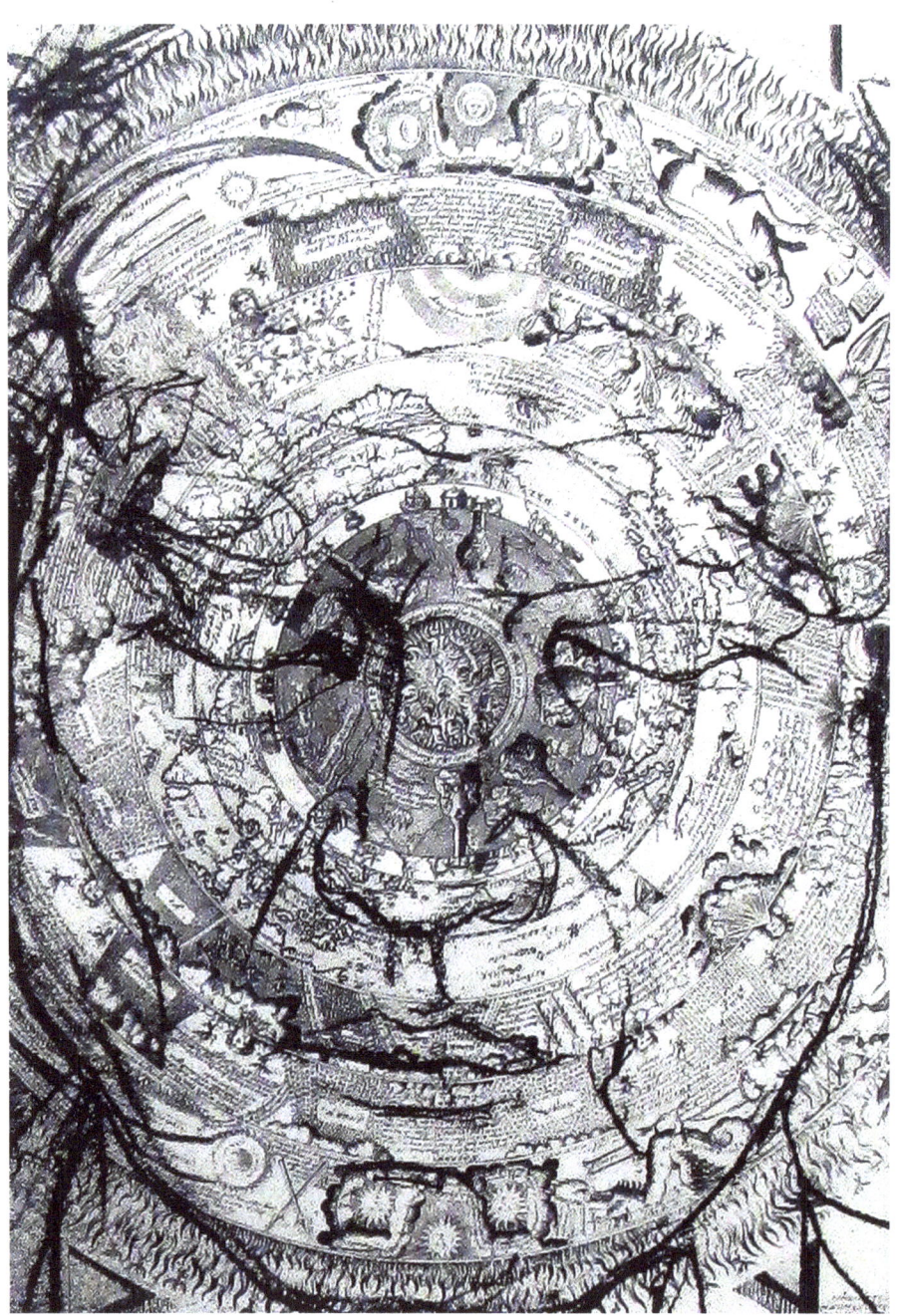

Maelstrom
pencil, charcoal, digital
19" x 13"

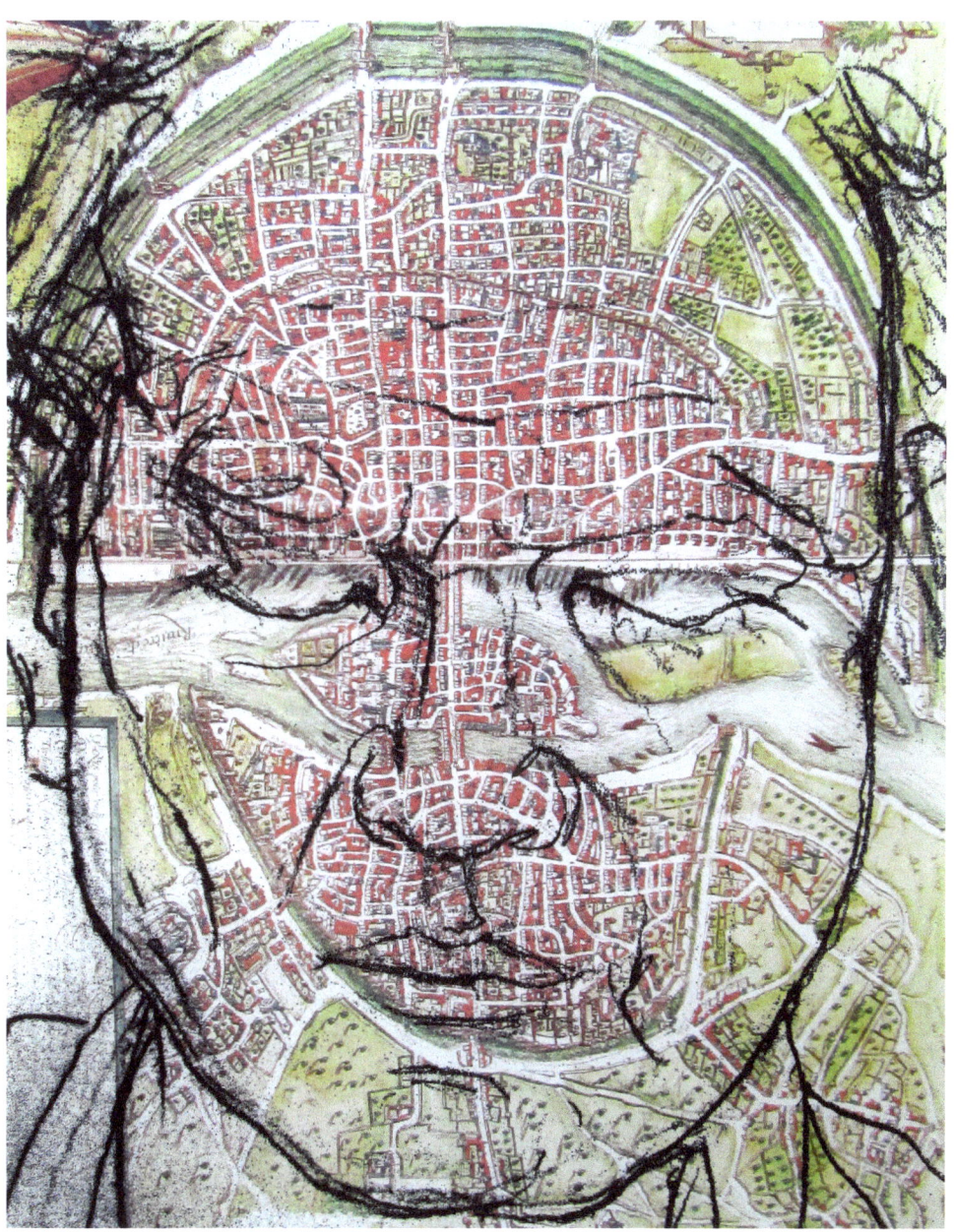

Traveler
pencil, charcoal, digital
19" x 13"

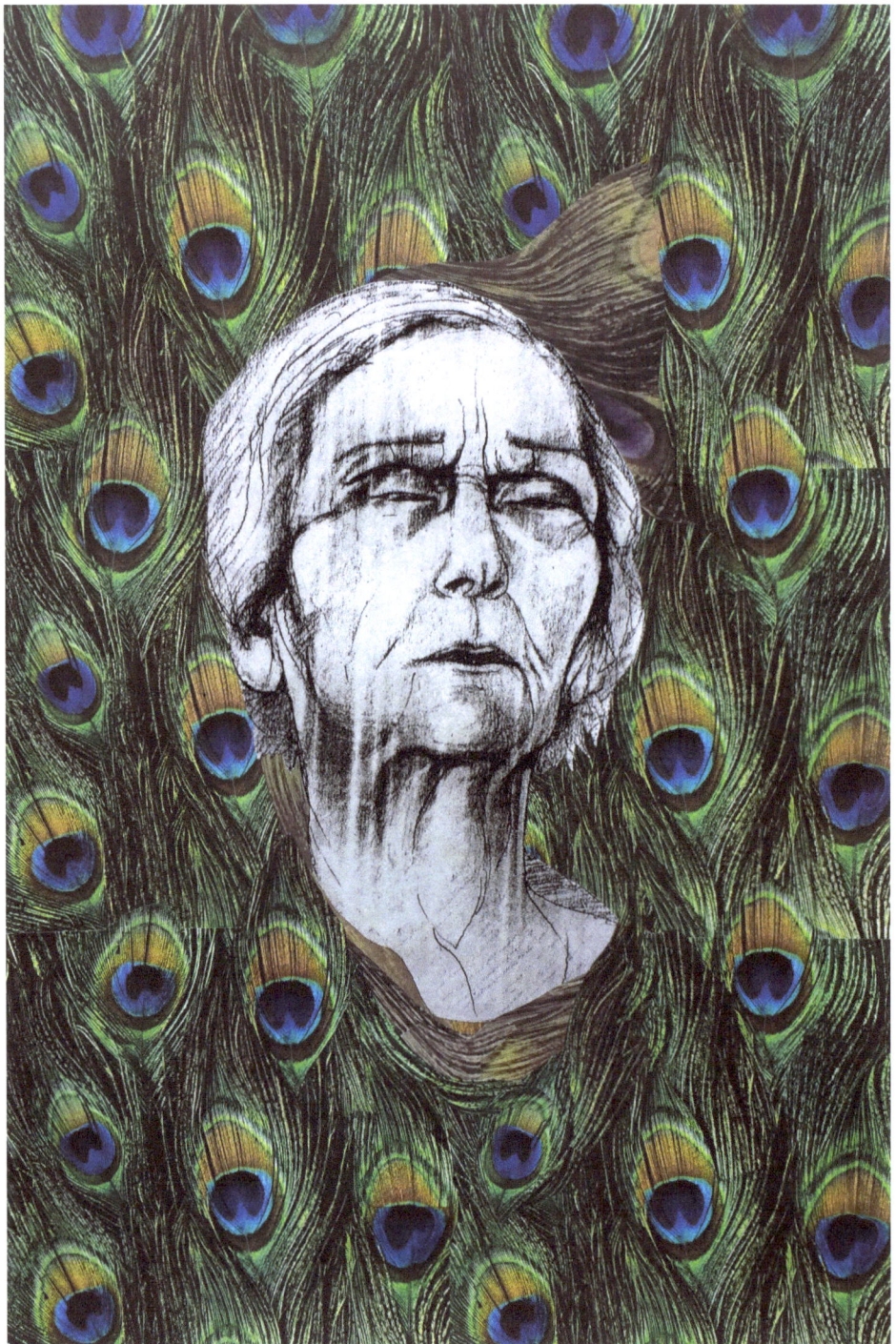

Passage
pencil, digital, decorative paper, collage
24" x 16"

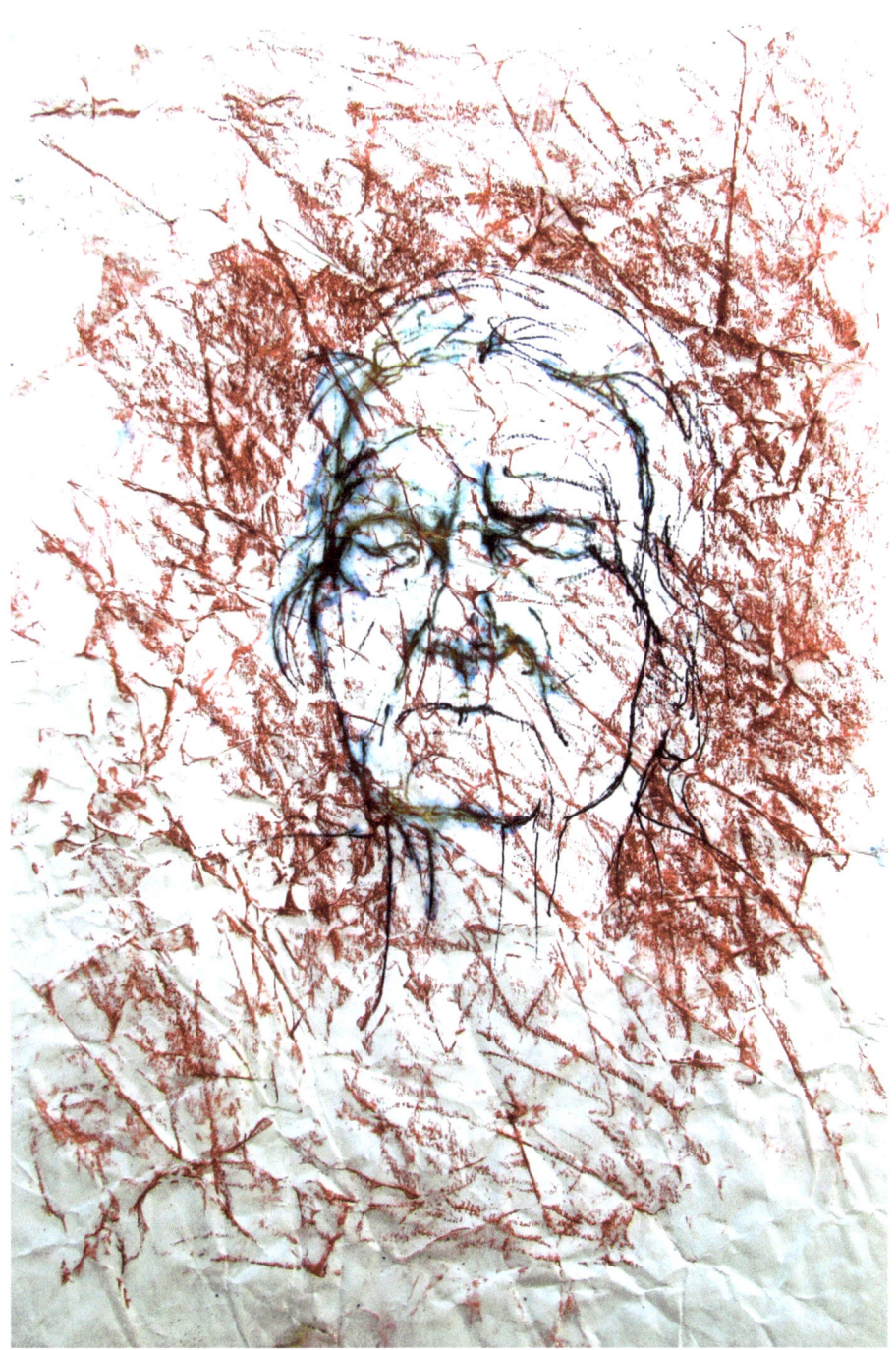

Disinterred
pencil, digital, conte crayon, earth on paper,
17" x 14"

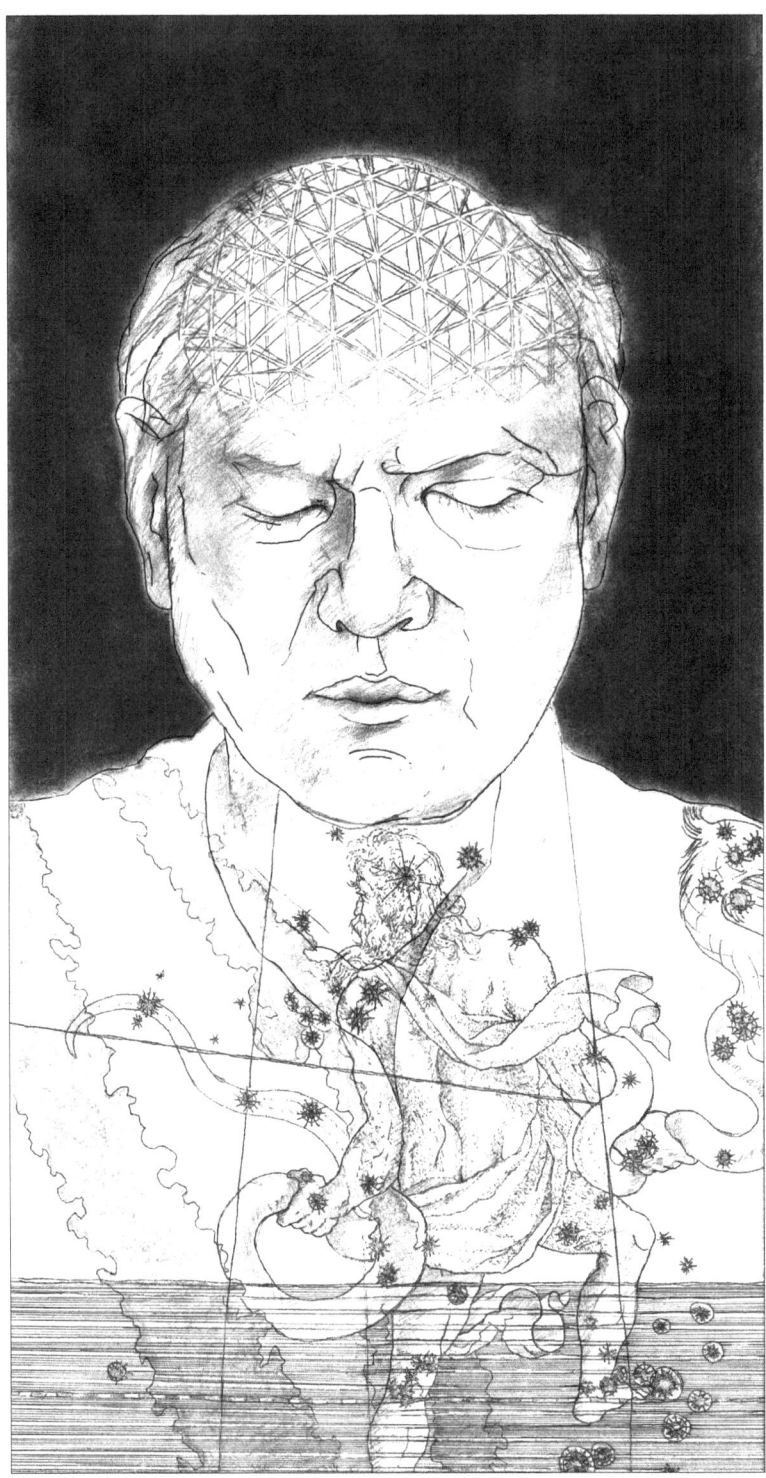

Ancestor, detail
pencil, digital, decorative paper, collage
24" x 16"

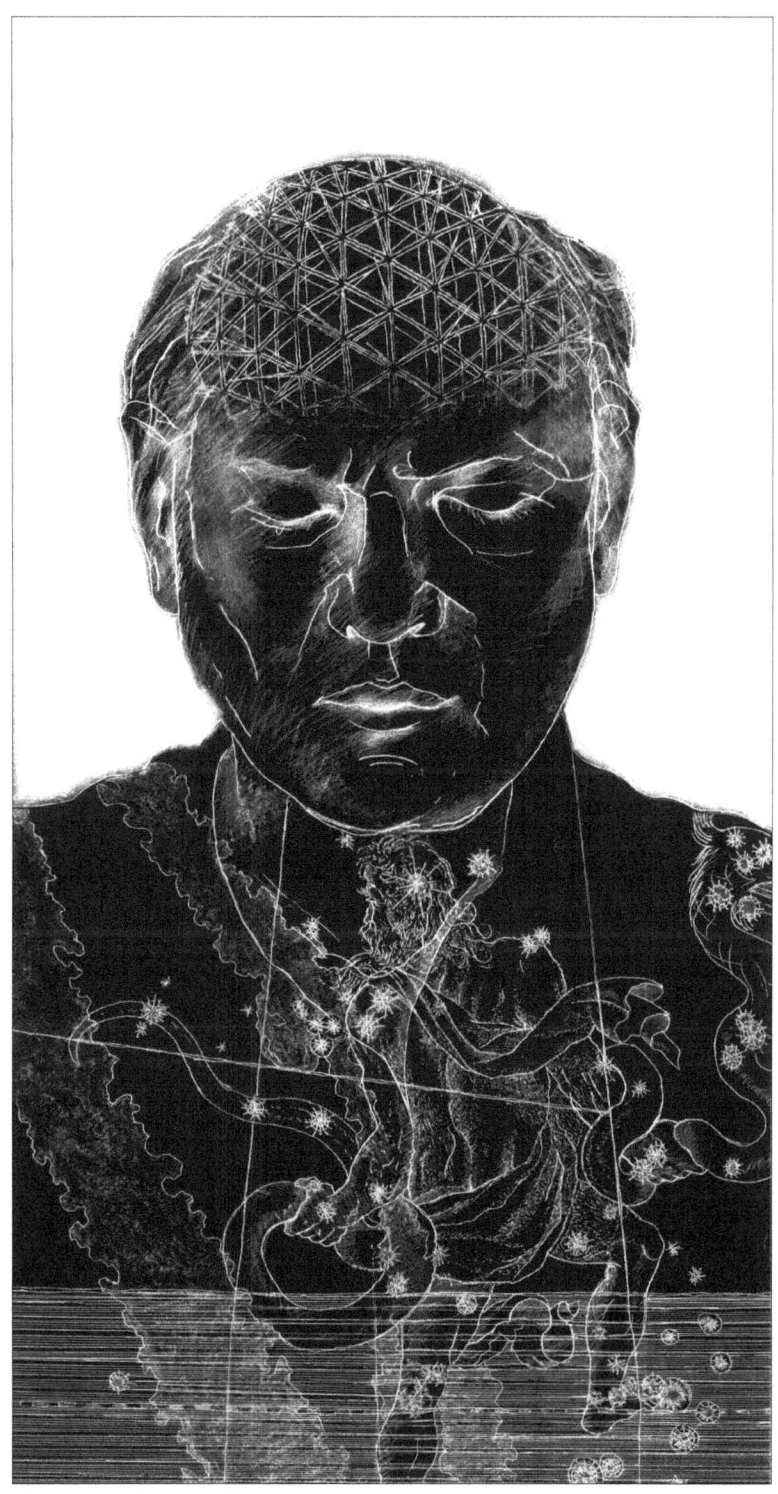

Ancestor II, detail
pencil, digital, decorative paper, collage
24" x 16"

Chapter 4

High Flow

LIKE A PLUME OF INK released into water, my high flow portraits are a natural and welcome extension of my traditional portraiture and "Mutations" series. The high flow portraits further broaden the psychological and aesthetic explorations of my subjects. In these portraits, I combine my traditional paintings with abstract and expressive flowing paint.

At times, I achieve this by cutting out the detail of the head and shoulders from a larger New Media print. I then collage the image onto my high flow paintings and rework these pieces with additional paint. I may alter the New Media print digitally, as in *The Sorceress* and/or employ multiple prints, as in *Twins*.

In another high flow methodology, I abandon collage, and pour these paints directly over New Media portraits, either on panel or canvas. This application is used in works such as *Vapors*, *Sara's Dream*, and *Howard's Ghost*. In these experimental pieces, the poured paint carries the subject into unexpected realms. In *Ghost*, the flowing paint verges on obliterating the subject entirely.

Through these approaches I attempt to expand the expressive spectrum of portraiture, unleashing the ephemeral and sublime.

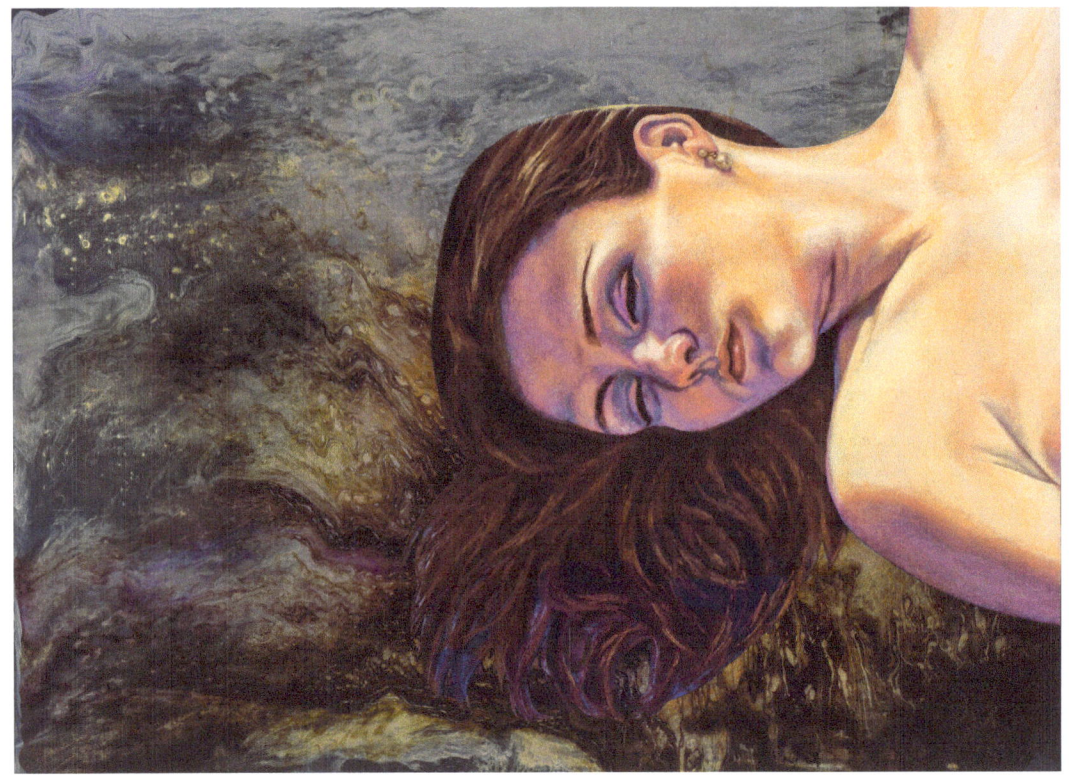

The River
oil, egg tempera, New Media, acrylic, collage on canvas, 18" x 24"

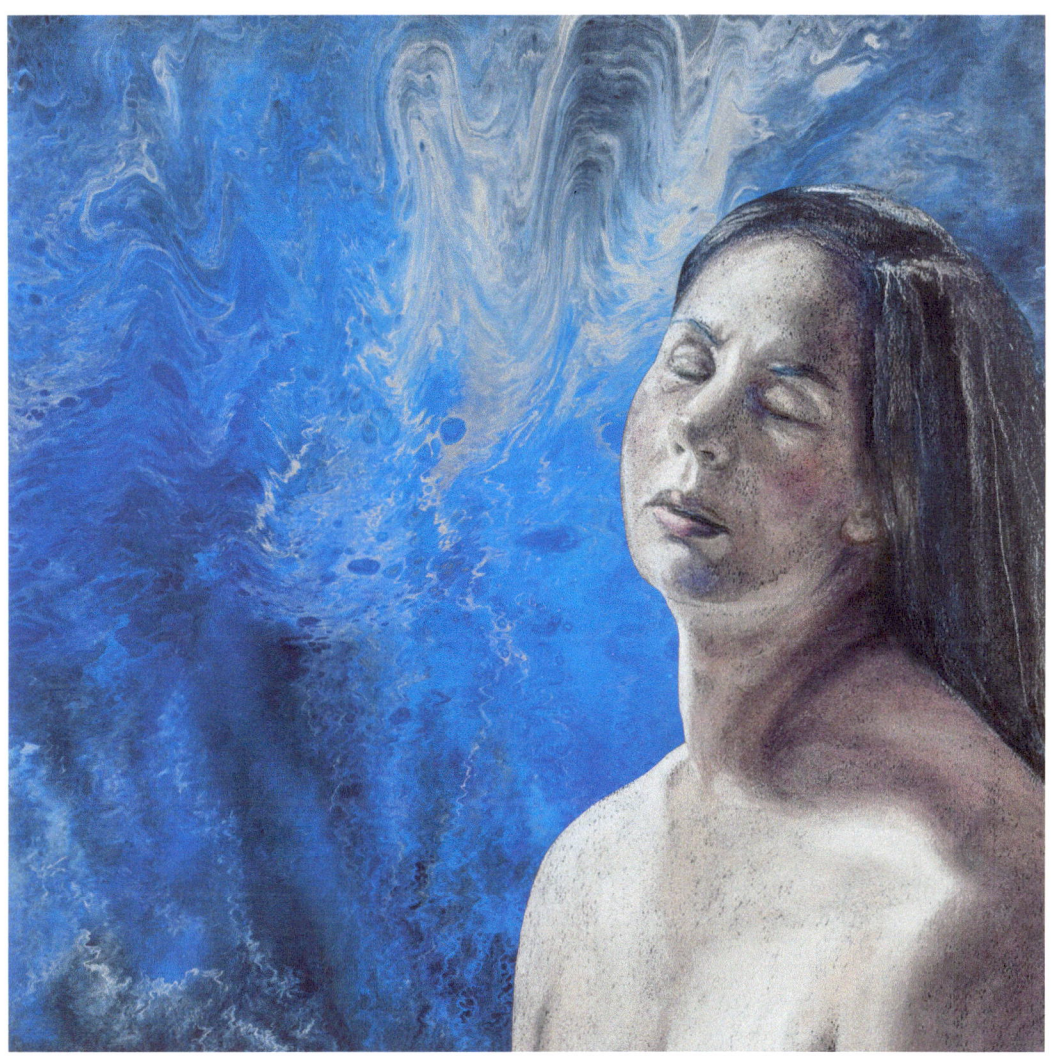

Leda
pastel, New Media, acrylic, collage on canvas, 18" x 17"

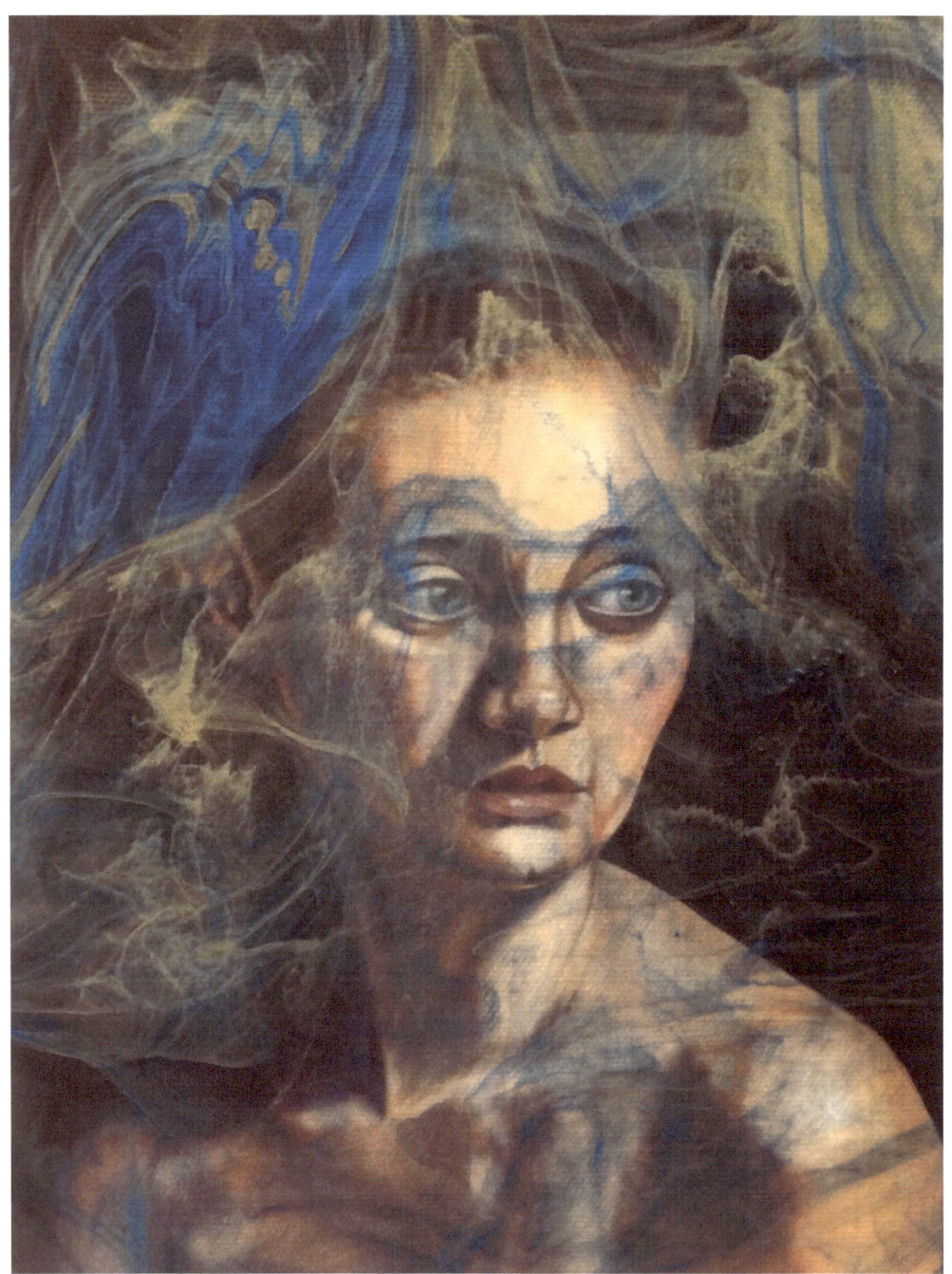

Sara's Dream
oil, egg tempera, New Media, acrylic on canvas, 16" x 12"

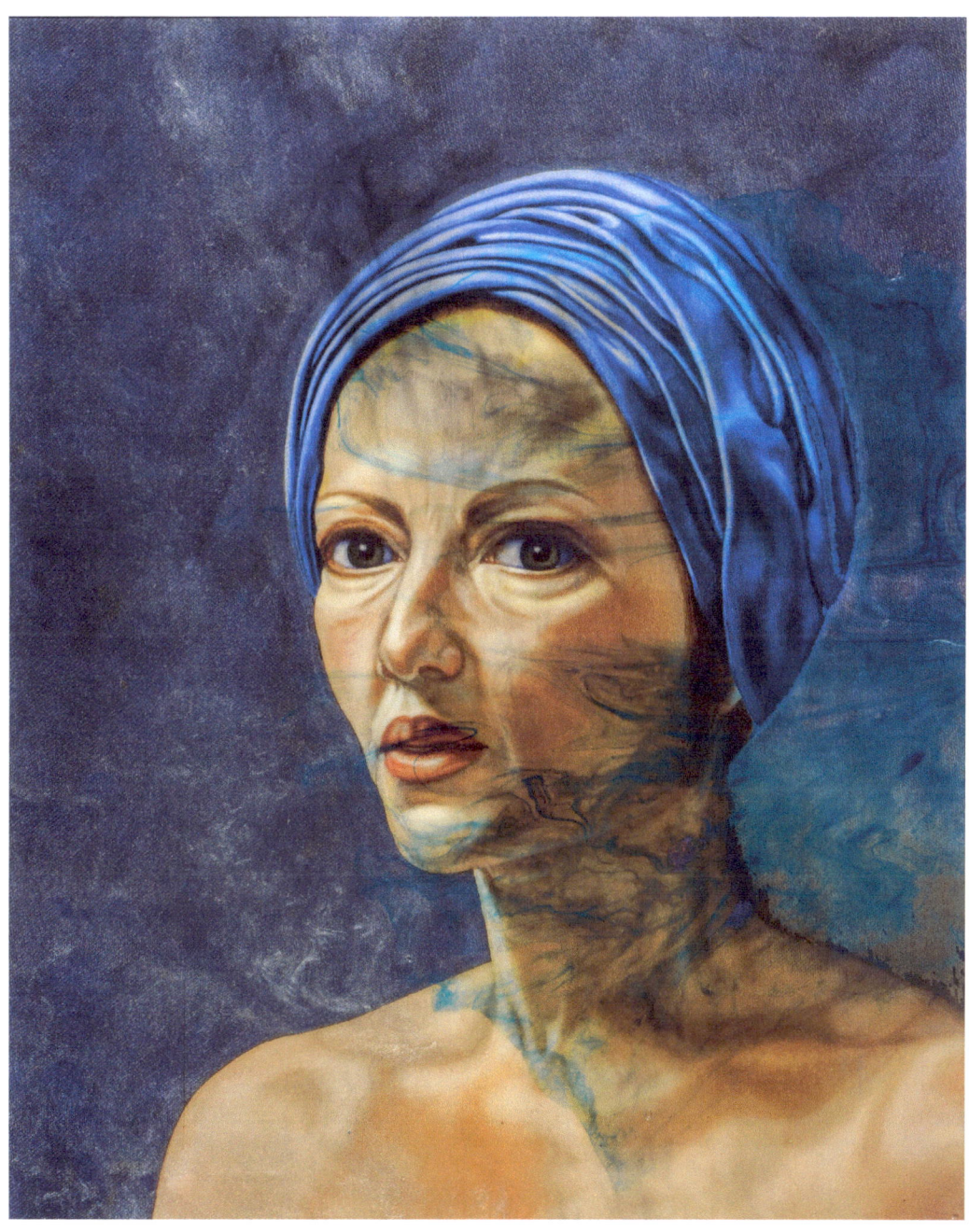

Vapors
oil, egg tempera, New Media, acrylic on canvas, 24" x 18"

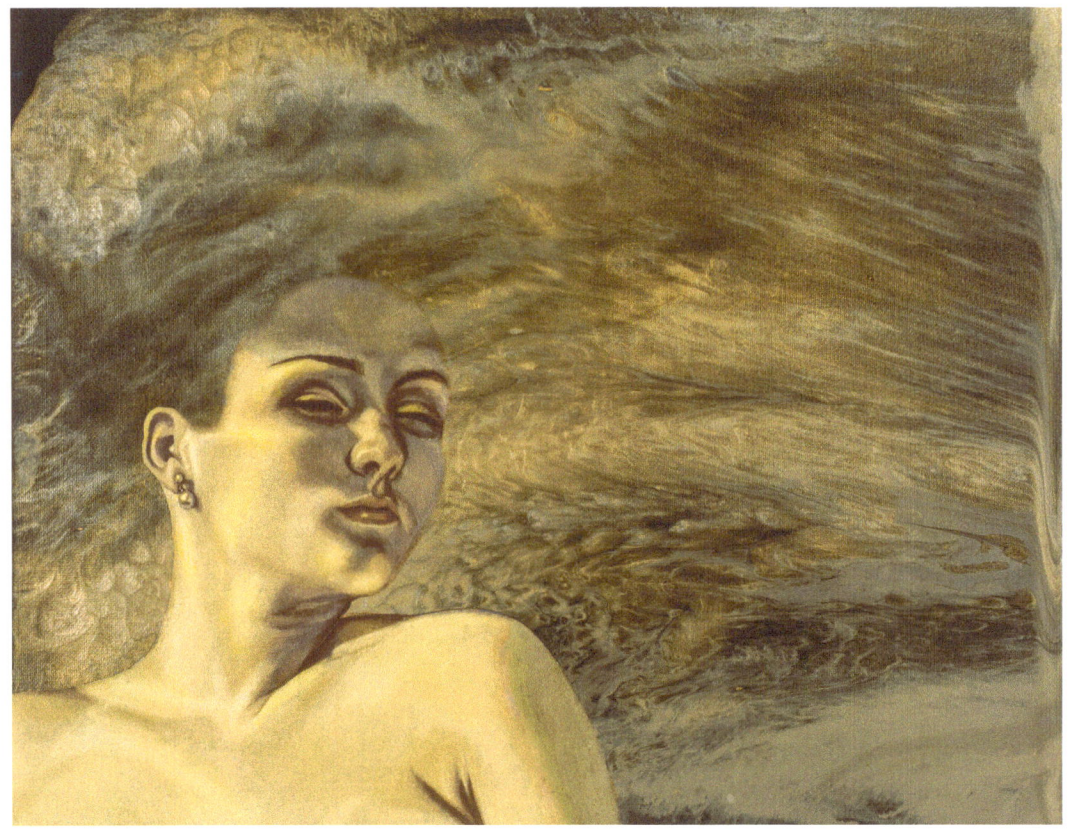

Sorceress
oil, egg tempera, New Media, acrylic, collage on canvas, 18" x 24"

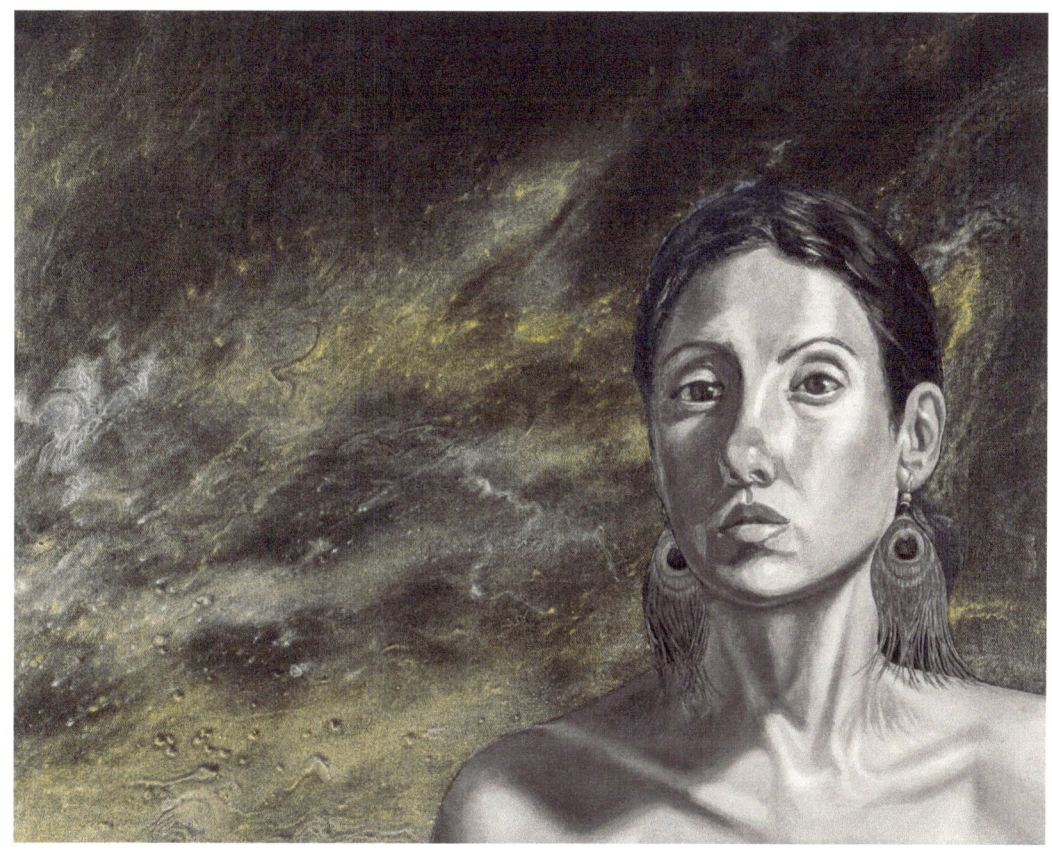

Midnight
oil, egg tempera, New Media, acrylic, collage on canvas, 18" x 24"

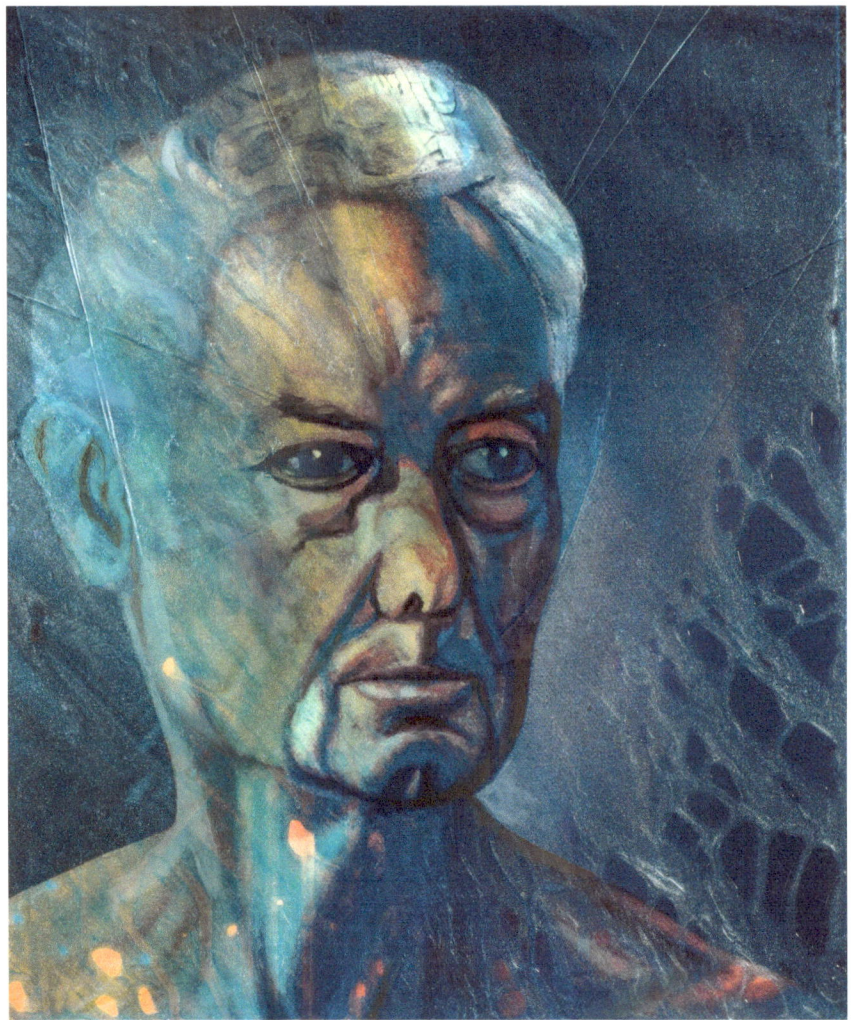

Howard's Ghost
oil, egg tempera, New Media, acrylic on canvas, 16" x 16"

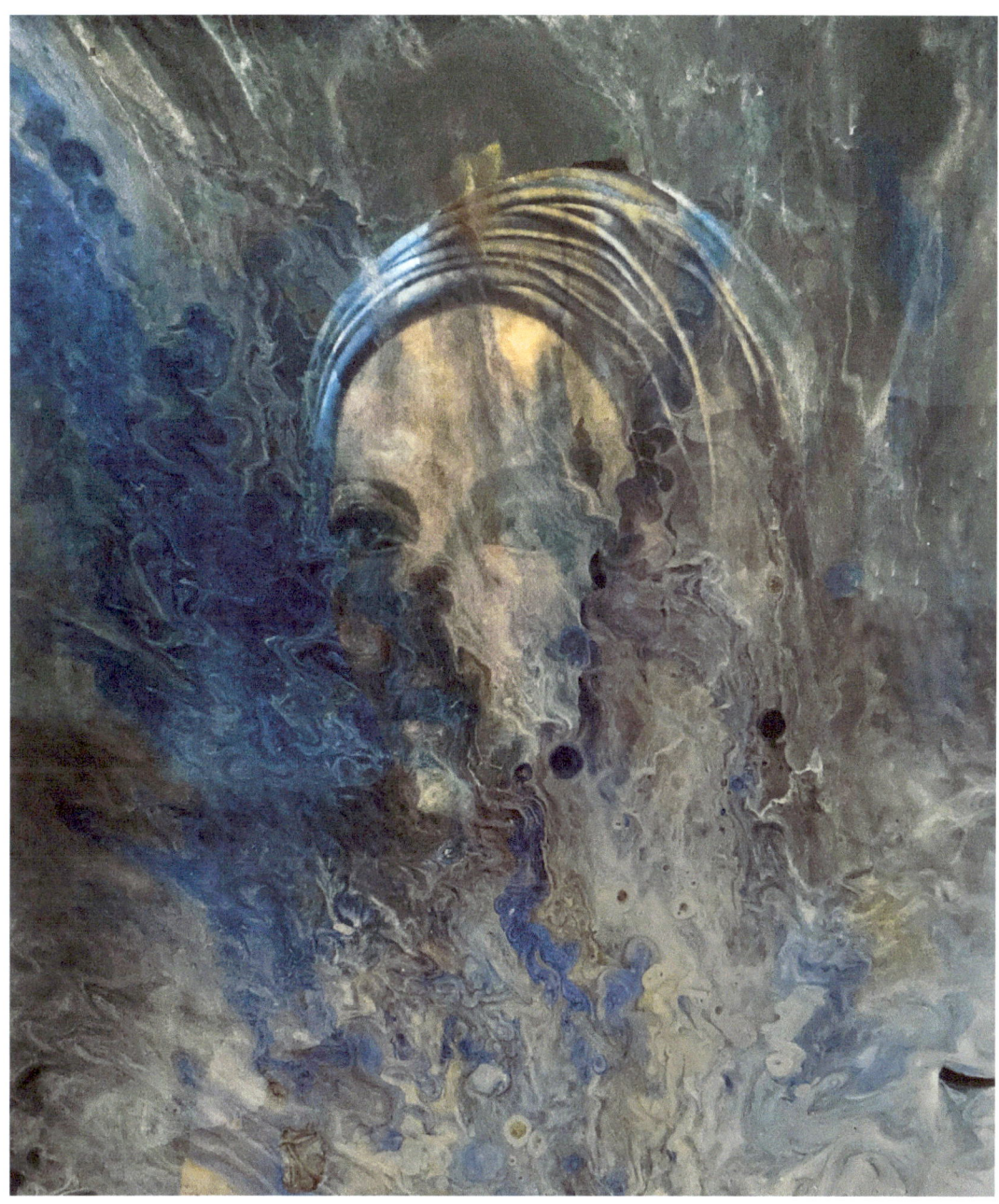

Ghost
oil, egg tempera, New Media, acrylic on canvas, 24" x 18"

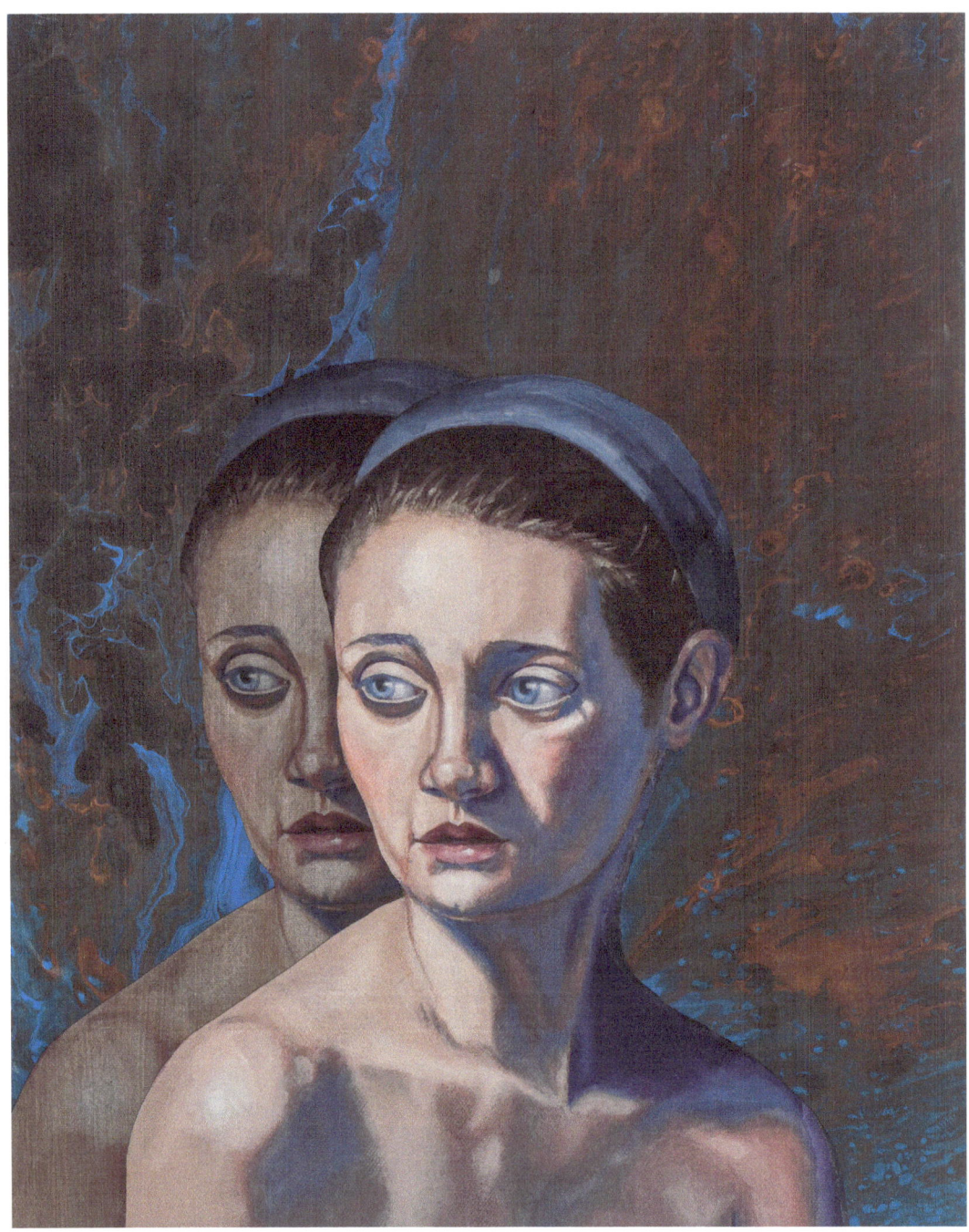

Twins
oil, egg tempera, New Media, collage, acrylic on canvas
24" x 18"

Chapter 5

Suminagashi
& Decorative Paper

THROUGHOUT MY CAREER, I have always been in search of the synergy, synthesis, and/or juxtaposition of abstract and/or patterned surfaces, in tandem with realistic representation. This is exemplified in *Embrace*, a New Media image created from my earlier egg tempera and oil painting, *Lovers*.

The use of decorative paper is a natural extension of my original high flow paintings and passion for textile design. My use of marbleized paper meshes with an ongoing interest in fractals, Abstract Expressionism, and high flow painting. Thus, I resonate not only with the complex and abstract beauty of textiles, but also with the random and expressive quality of meandering paint.

This brings me to the discovery of Suminagashi paper.* Imagine my surprise and thrill, as I entered my local art supply store, to discover these exquisite sheets. These extraordinary papers were hanging on dowels for sale! I felt lightheaded.... These papers fit like a hand in a glove, meshing perfectly with my own creative proclivities and quest.

In this series I employ a variety of decorative and marbleized papers in pieces such as *After Image* and *Drowning*, as well as Suminagashi papers in portraits such as *Skye II* and *Bella*. I am humbled by the beauty of these materials and the qualities they bring to my work.

*(Suminagashi papers originated in China over 2,000 years ago and were created in Japan by Shinto priests as early as the 12th century.)

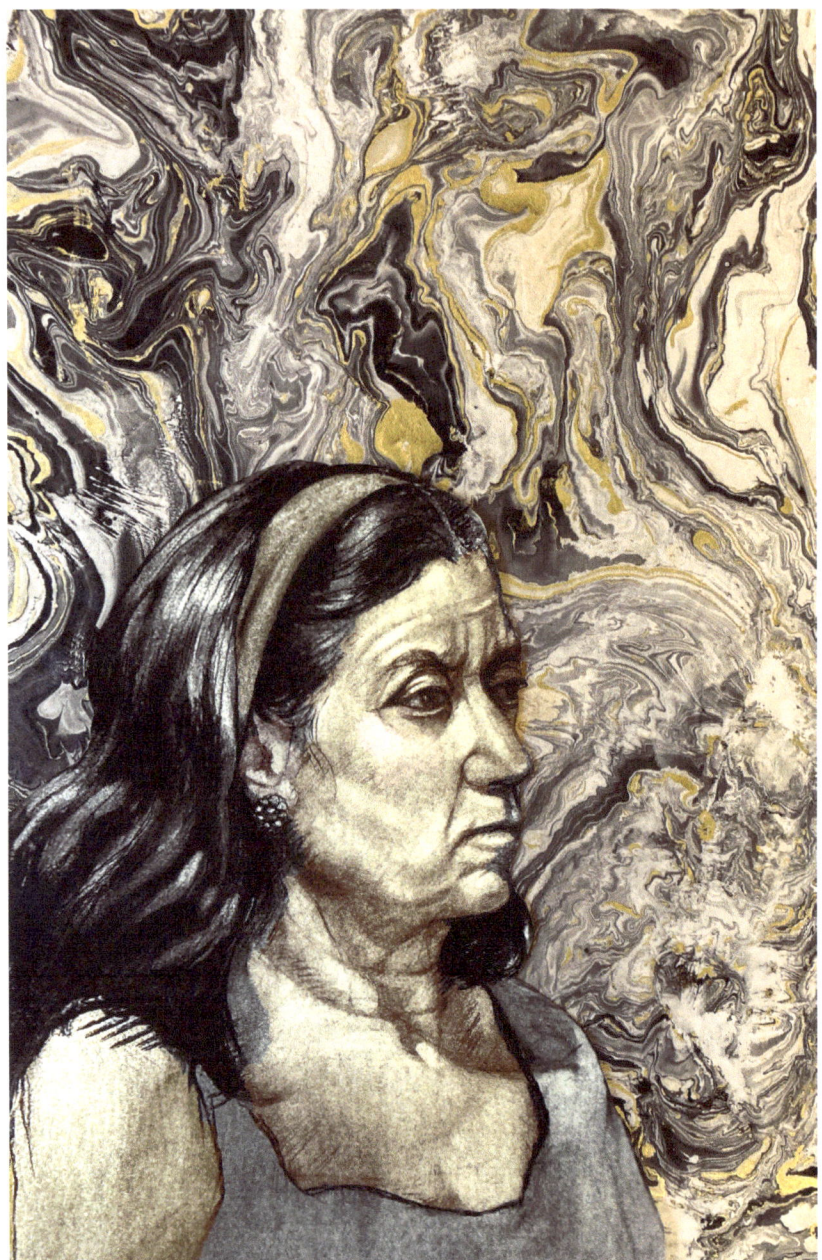

Hazel
charcoal, digital, collage on marbelized paper
44" x 32"

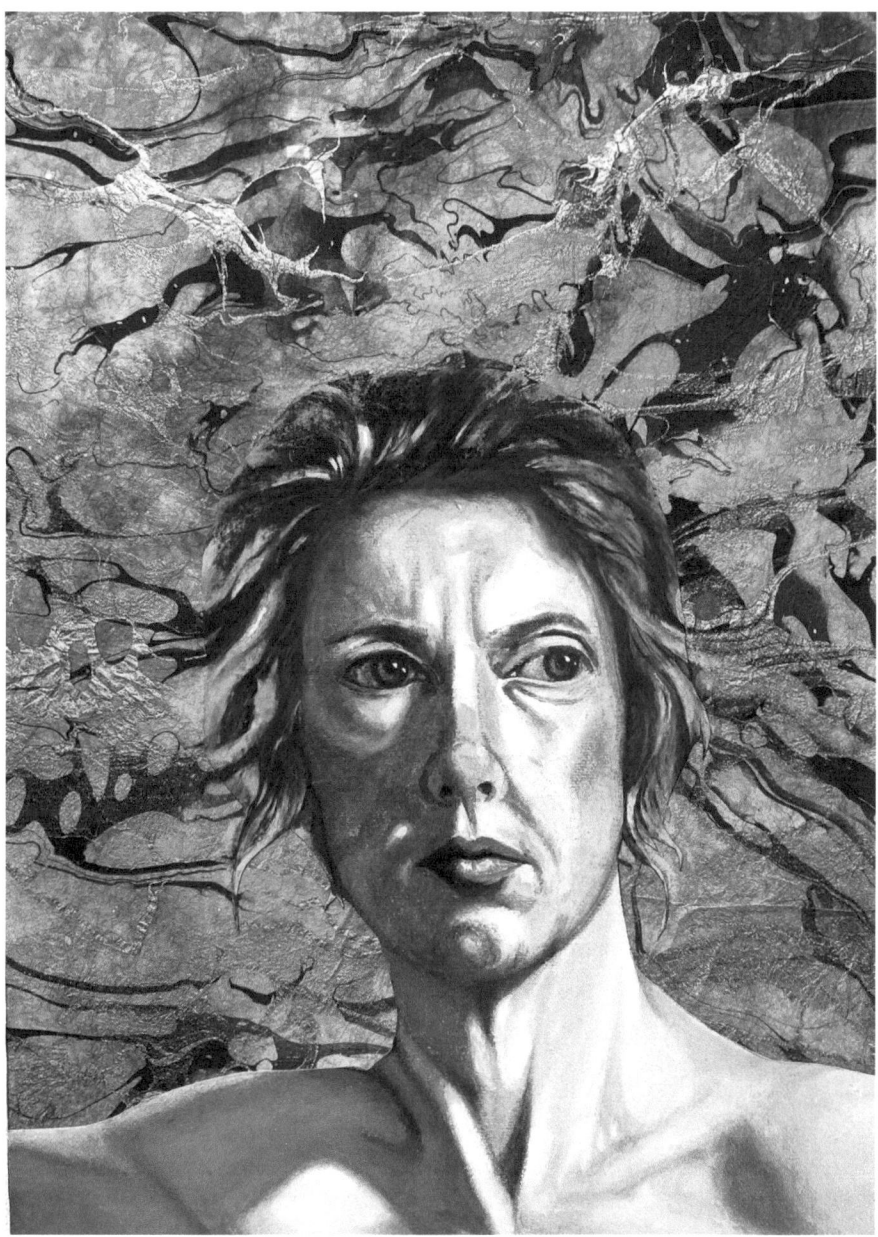

Uriel
oil, egg tempera, digital, pastel on Suminagashi paper
19" x 13"

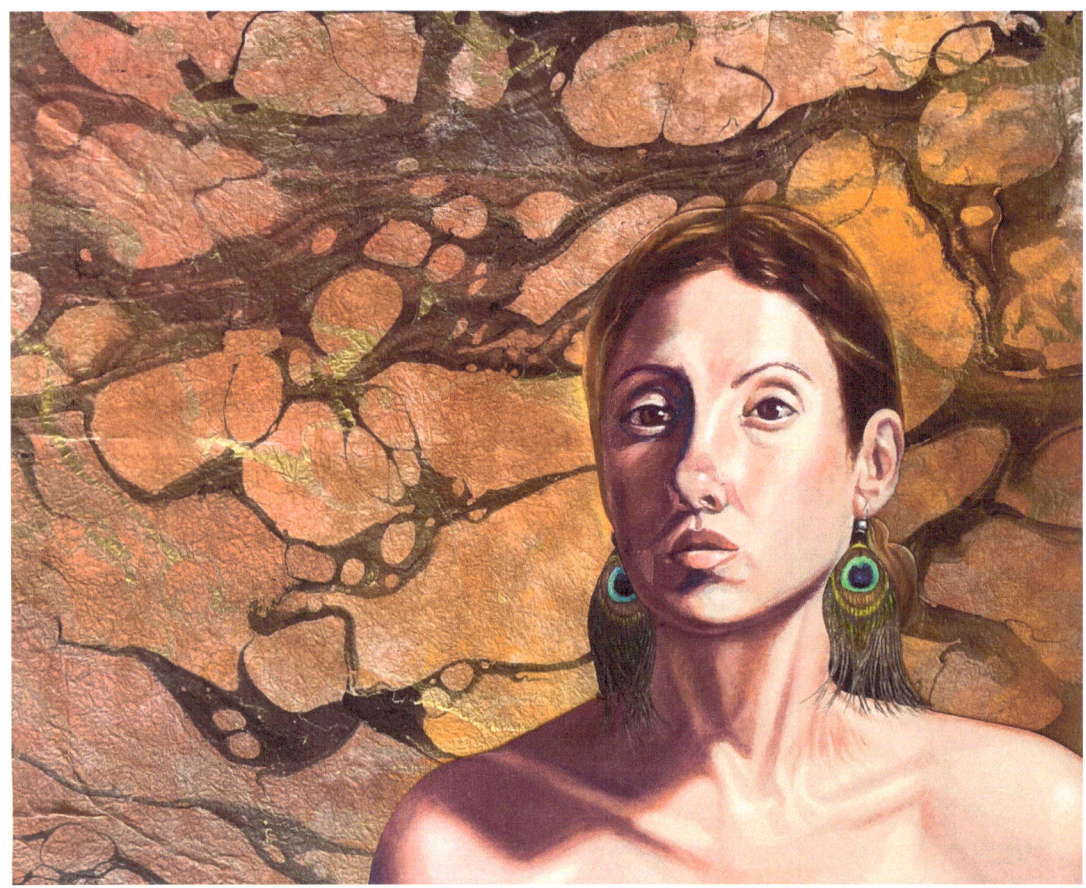

Bella
oil, pastel, New Media, collage on Suminagashi paper
23" x 19"

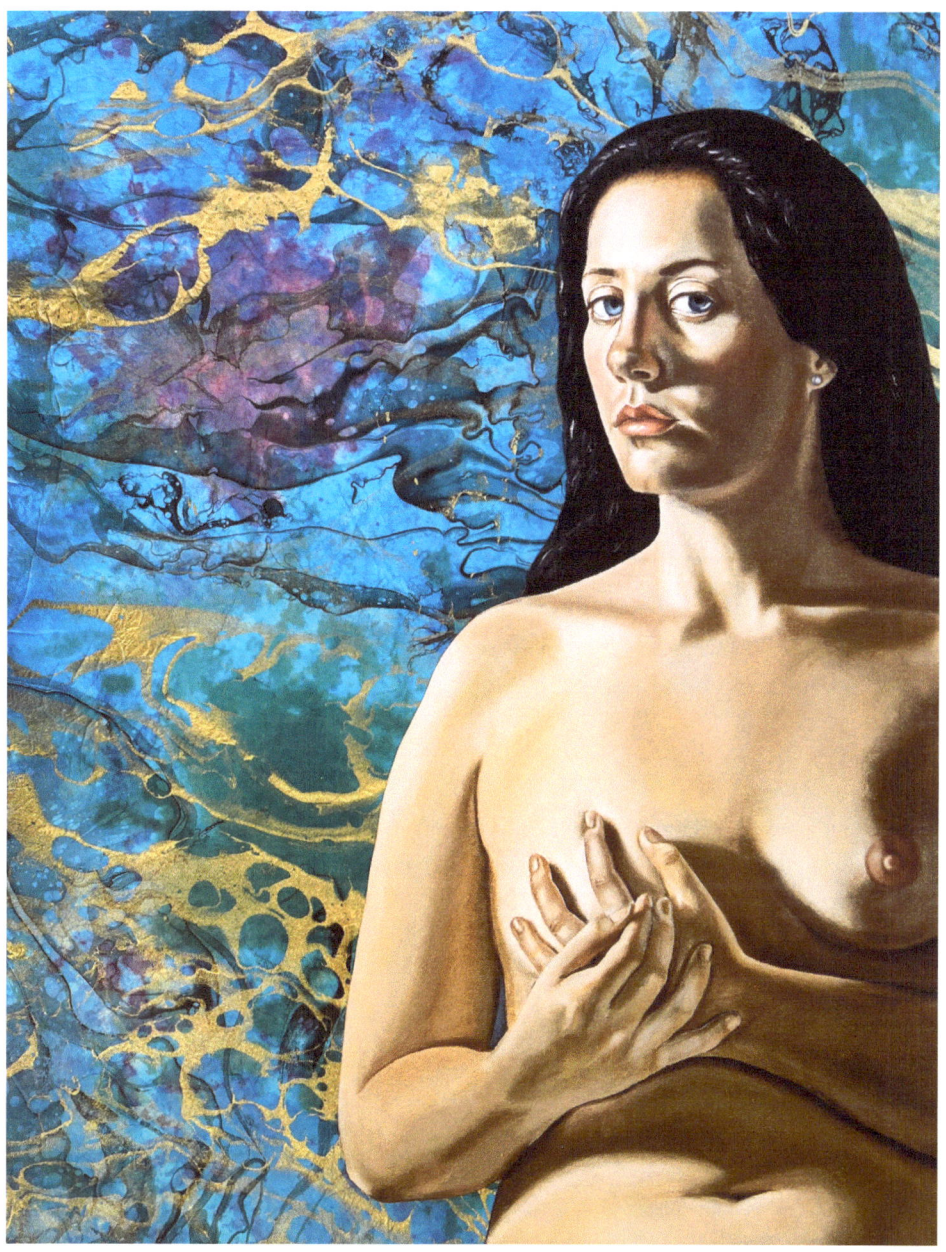

Skye II
oil, egg tempera, New Media, acrylic on Suminagashi paper
24" x 18"

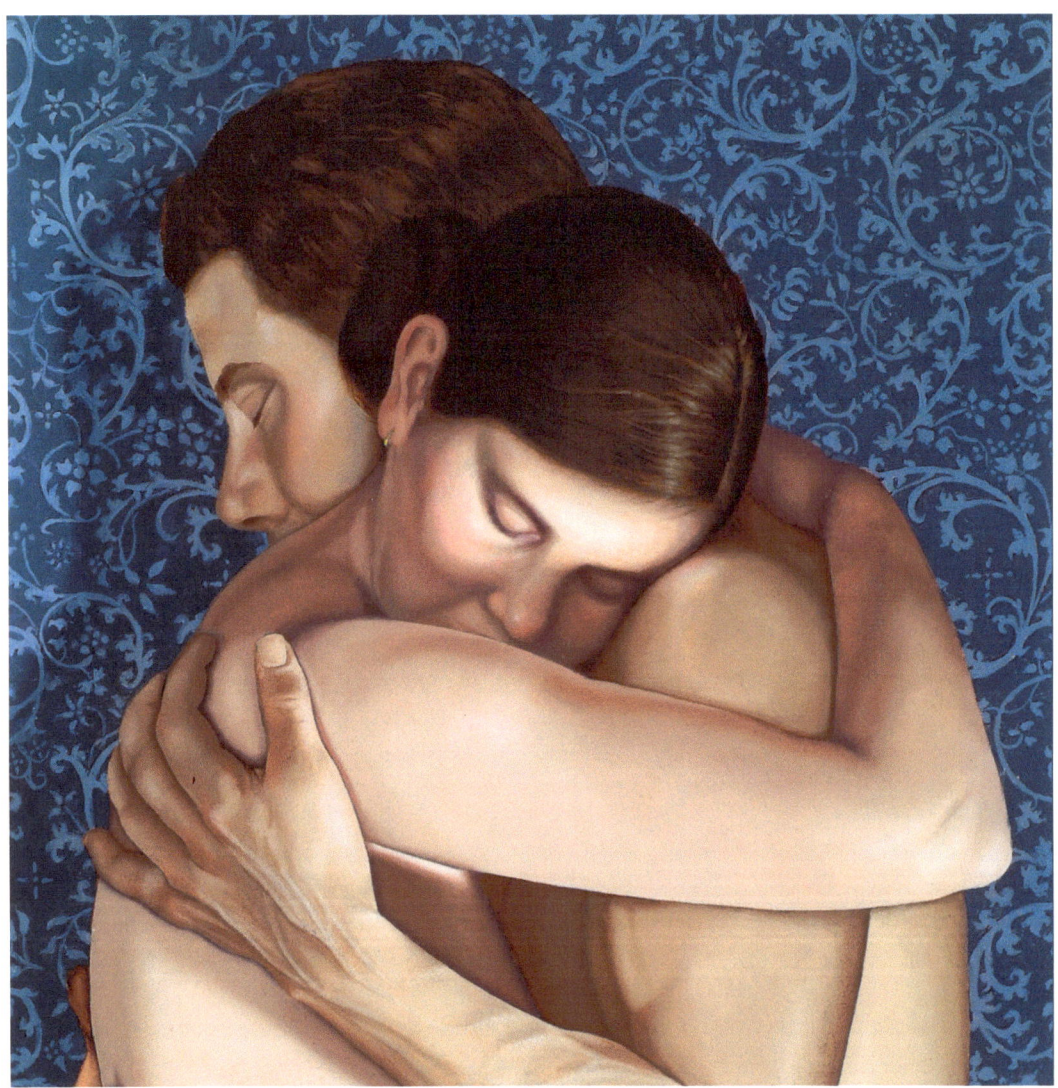

Embrace
oil and egg tempera on canvas, New Media
32" x 32"

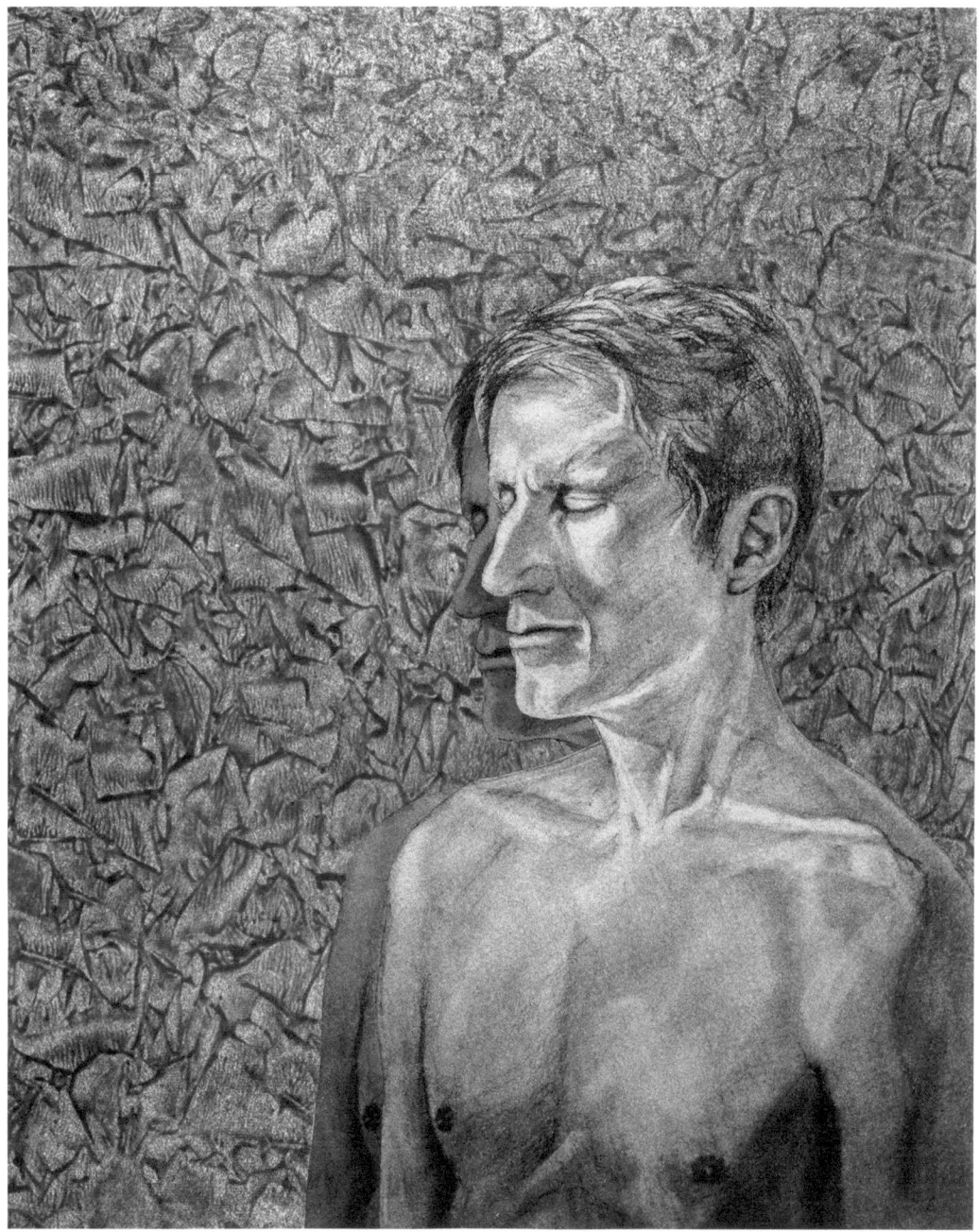

After Image
pencil, digital, charcoal, collage, on decorative paper
24" x 18"

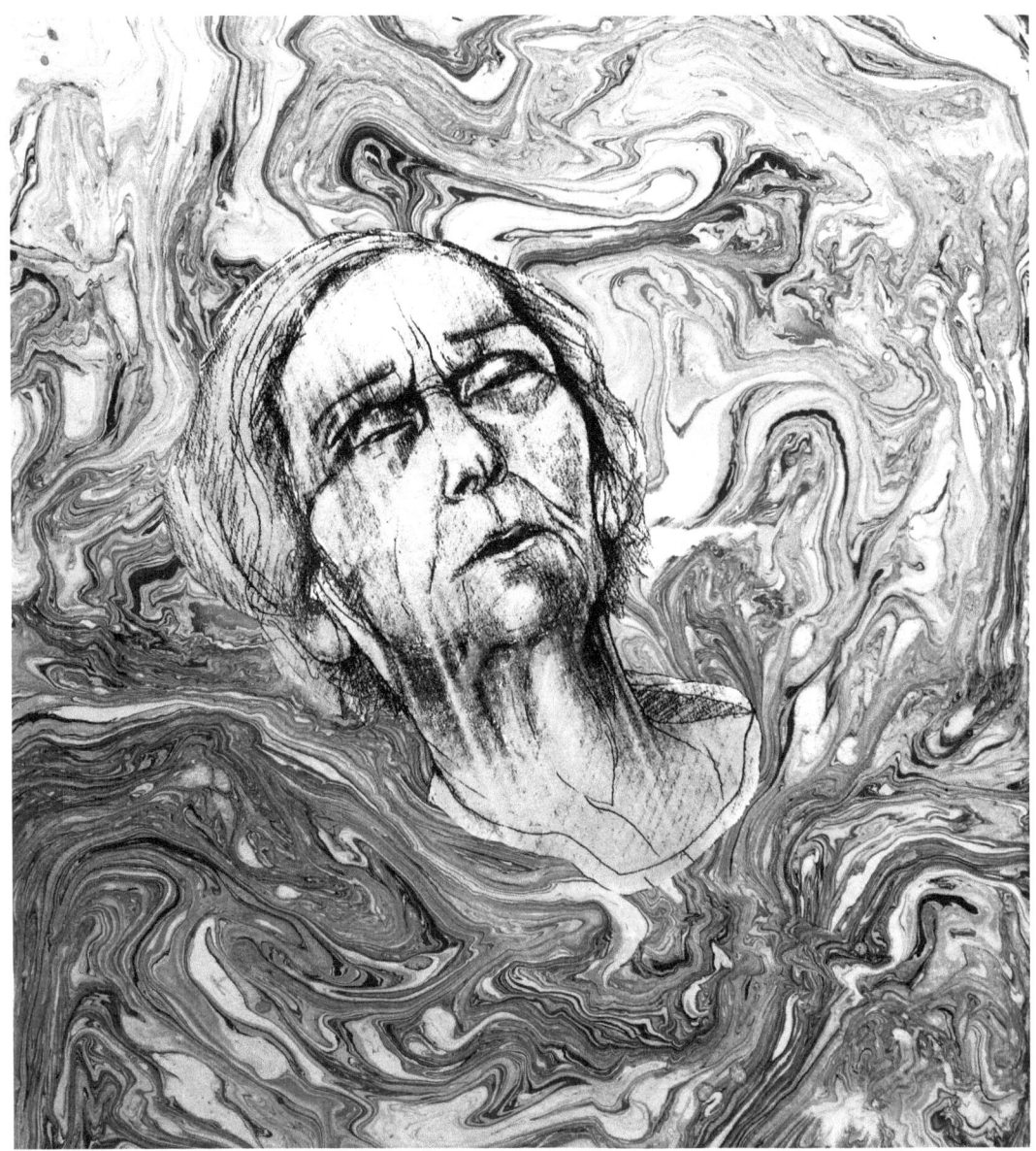

Passage II
pencil, digital, collage on marbelized paper
24" x 20"

All the world's a stage,
And all the men and women merely players;
They have their exits and their entrances;
And one man in his time plays many parts,
His acts being seven ages. At first the infant,
. . . And then the lover,
Sighing like furnace, with a woeful ballad
Made to his mistress' eyebrow. Then a soldier,
Full of strange oaths, and bearded like the pard,
Jealous in honour, sudden and quick in quarrel,
Seeking the bubble reputation
Even in the cannon's mouth. And then the justice,
. . . full of wise saws and modern instances;
And so he [she] plays [the] part. The sixth age shifts . . .
Turning again toward childish treble, pipes
And whistles in his sound. Last scene of all,
That ends this strange eventful history,
Is . . . mere oblivion;
Sans teeth, sans eyes, sans taste, sans everything.

William Shakespeare
(from *As You Like It*, spoken by Jaques)

Biographical Notes

Rebecca Gabriel is an Art Market International Gold List Award Artist. She holds an MFA from the University of Massachusetts in Amherst, and has also studied in Europe through Naropa University, Denver, CO.

Gabriel was interviewed for *Art Market international Magazine,* Issue #46, April 2020. The magazine listed this interview as one of its most influential articles. She participated in the XII Florence Biennale, 2019, in Italy. Her work has been exhibited at the Schneider Museum of Art, Ashland, OR; Denver Art Museum, CO; De Cordova Museum, MA; Oakland Museum, CA; Herbert F. Johnson Museum, Cornell University, NY; etc. A retrospective of Gabriel's work was held at the Rogue Gallery and Art Center in Medford, Oregon.

Her art has received numerous awards, such as: First Award, Juror Henry Hopkins, "All California Art Exhibition"; Finalist in *Artist's Magazine;* and Jurors Choice award in the "Human Form" exhibit, Newport Visual Art Center, OR.

Gabriel's work was selected for extended loan in the Executive Chairman's office at the National Endowment for the Arts in Washington, D. C. She is represented by Gallerie Karon, Ashland, OR; Verum Ultimum Art Gallery, Portland, OR; and Israeli Art Market.

Rebecca Gabriel's published monograph, *A Woman's Journey – A Life in Art*, has received critical acclaim. Dr. Jean Houston asserts "Rebecca Gabriel gives us potent insight...into the artist at critical times." Art critic, Robert C. Morgan, writes, "Her ingenuity in perceiving her subjects...depends on an ability to understand painting as a language."

Rebecca Gabriel has been awarded a University of Massachusetts Fellowship in Painting, as well as a Haines Foundation Grant. Her work is featured in the following publications: *Art Market International, Calyx, Studio Visit, American Artwork*, and *World of Art MOMA.*

Gabriel is a participating artist in the Israeli Art Market Group Exhibition 2020 and 2021, and was a contributing artist in the 2021 national juried exhibition, "Portrayed," at the d'Art Center in Norfolk, Virginia. She is a featured artist in Biafarin and Gallerium's online exhibitions: Children-21; Emotions; Anti-War 2022; Cancer-22; and Gallerium Artists' Prize 2022. Gabriel has shown consistently at Verum Ultimum Art Gallery and is a featured artist in its Chasing Ghosts exhibitions.

Her work was chosen by *Art Market International* magazine for its Gold List Artist Award issue of 2021, as well as the exhibition, "Self-Expression—The Artist's Truth" at MVA Gallery in Bethlehem, PA in 2022.

Links

www.rebeccagabriel.com
https://en.wikipedia.org/wiki/Rebecca_Gabriel
http://artmarketmag.com
https://www.biafarin.com/p/artist.html?name=rebecca-gabriel
https://www.verumultimumartgallery.com/artists
https://www.facebook.com/profile.php?id=100009315379764
https://www.instagram.com/rgabrielartist/

John Seed is author of *Disrupted Realism*, as well as *My Art World*. He has been a contributing art critic for *The Huffington Post, American Art Collector* and *Arts of Asia*. Seed's artwork is represented by the Larry Gagosian Gallery. He is faculty Emeritus in studio art, art theory, and art criticism at the Art Center College of Design in Pasadena, and the Laguna College of Art. John Seed currently serves on the board of the Sam Francis Foundation in Pasadena, CA.

www.ingramcontent.com/pod-product-compliance
Lightning Source LLC
Chambersburg PA
CBHW040323190526
45162CB00007B/62